HEART OF DARKNESS

Joseph Conrad

SPARK PUBLISHING

SPARKNOTES is a registered trademark of SparkNotes LLC

Spark Publishing
A Division of Barnes & Noble
120 Fifth Avenue
New York, NY 10011
www.sparknotes.com

ISBN-13: 978-1-4114-0370-3
ISBN-10: 1-4114-0370-3

Please submit changes or report errors to www.sparknotes.com/errors.

Printed in the United States.

10 9 8 7 6

CONTENTS

CONTEXT

JOSEPH CONRAD DID NOT BEGIN TO LEARN ENGLISH until he was twenty-one years old. He was born Jozef Teodor Konrad Korzeniowski on December 3, 1857, in the Polish Ukraine. When Conrad was quite young, his father was exiled to Siberia on suspicion of plotting against the Russian government. After the death of the boy's mother, Conrad's father sent him to his mother's brother in Kraków to be educated, and Conrad never again saw his father. He traveled to Marseilles when he was seventeen and spent the next twenty years as a sailor. He signed on to an English ship in 1878, and eight years later he became a British subject. In 1889, he began his first novel, *Almayer's Folly*, and began actively searching for a way to fulfill his boyhood dream of traveling to the Congo. He took command of a steamship in the Belgian Congo in 1890, and his experiences in the Congo came to provide the outline for *Heart of Darkness*. Conrad's time in Africa wreaked havoc on his health, however, and he returned to England to recover. He returned to sea twice before finishing *Almayer's Folly* in 1894 and wrote several other books, including one about Marlow called *Youth: A Narrative* before beginning *Heart of Darkness* in 1898. He wrote most of his other major works—including *Lord Jim*, which also features Marlow; *Nostromo;* and *The Secret Agent,* as well as several collaborations with Ford Madox Ford—during the following two decades. Conrad died in 1924.

Conrad's works, *Heart of Darkness* in particular, provide a bridge between Victorian values and the ideals of modernism. Like their Victorian predecessors, these novels rely on traditional ideas of heroism, which are nevertheless under constant attack in a changing world and in places far from England. Women occupy traditional roles as arbiters of domesticity and morality, yet they are almost never present in the narrative; instead, the concepts of "home" and "civilization" exist merely as hypocritical ideals, meaningless to men for whom survival is in constant doubt. While the threats that Conrad's characters face are concrete ones—illness, violence, conspiracy—they nevertheless acquire a philosophical character. Like much of the best modernist literature produced in the early decades of the twentieth century, *Heart of Darkness* is as much about alienation, confusion, and profound doubt as it is about imperialism.

Imperialism is nevertheless at the center of *Heart of Darkness*. By the 1890s, most of the world's "dark places" had been placed at least nominally under European control, and the major European powers were stretched thin, trying to administer and protect massive, far-flung empires. Cracks were beginning to appear in the system: riots, wars, and the wholesale abandonment of commercial enterprises all threatened the white men living in the distant corners of empires. Things were clearly falling apart. *Heart of Darkness* suggests that this is the natural result when men are allowed to operate outside a social system of checks and balances: power, especially power over other human beings, inevitably corrupts. At the same time, this begs the question of whether it is possible to call an individual insane or wrong when he is part of a system that is so thoroughly corrupted and corrupting. *Heart of Darkness,* thus, at its most abstract level, is a narrative about the difficulty of understanding the world beyond the self, about the ability of one man to judge another.

Although *Heart of Darkness* was one of the first literary texts to provide a critical view of European imperial activities, it was initially read by critics as anything but controversial. While the book was generally admired, it was typically read either as a condemnation of a certain type of adventurer who could easily take advantage of imperialism's opportunities, or else as a sentimental novel reinforcing domestic values: Kurtz's Intended, who appears at the novella's conclusion, was roundly praised by turn-of-the-century reviewers for her maturity and sentimental appeal. Conrad's decision to set the book in a Belgian colony and to have Marlow work for a Belgian trading concern made it even easier for British readers to avoid seeing themselves reflected in *Heart of Darkness*. Although these early reactions seem ludicrous to a modern reader, they reinforce the novella's central themes of hypocrisy and absurdity.

PLOT OVERVIEW

HEART OF DARKNESS centers around Marlow, an introspective sailor, and his journey up the Congo River to meet Kurtz, reputed to be an idealistic man of great abilities. Marlow takes a job as a riverboat captain with the Company, a Belgian concern organized to trade in the Congo. As he travels to Africa and then up the Congo, Marlow encounters widespread inefficiency and brutality in the Company's stations. The native inhabitants of the region have been forced into the Company's service, and they suffer terribly from overwork and ill treatment at the hands of the Company's agents. The cruelty and squalor of imperial enterprise contrasts sharply with the impassive and majestic jungle that surrounds the white man's settlements, making them appear to be tiny islands amidst a vast darkness.

Marlow arrives at the Central Station, run by the general manager, an unwholesome, conspiratorial character. He finds that his steamship has been sunk and spends several months waiting for parts to repair it. His interest in Kurtz grows during this period. The manager and his favorite, the brickmaker, seem to fear Kurtz as a threat to their position. Kurtz is rumored to be ill, making the delays in repairing the ship all the more costly. Marlow eventually gets the parts he needs to repair his ship, and he and the manager set out with a few agents (whom Marlow calls pilgrims because of their strange habit of carrying long, wooden staves wherever they go) and a crew of cannibals on a long, difficult voyage up the river. The dense jungle and the oppressive silence make everyone aboard a little jumpy, and the occasional glimpse of a native village or the sound of drums works the pilgrims into a frenzy.

Marlow and his crew come across a hut with stacked firewood, together with a note saying that the wood is for them but that they should approach cautiously. Shortly after the steamer has taken on the firewood, it is surrounded by a dense fog. When the fog clears, the ship is attacked by an unseen band of natives, who fire arrows from the safety of the forest. The African helmsman is killed before Marlow frightens the natives away with the ship's steam whistle. Not long after, Marlow and his companions arrive at Kurtz's Inner Station, expecting to find him dead, but a half-crazed Russian trader, who meets them as they come ashore, assures them that everything is fine and informs them that he is the one who left the wood. The Russian claims that Kurtz has enlarged his mind and cannot be subjected to the same moral judgments as normal people. Apparently, Kurtz has established himself as a god with the natives and has gone on brutal raids in the surrounding territory in search of ivory. The collection of severed heads adorning the fence posts around the station attests to his "methods." The pilgrims bring Kurtz out of the station-house on a stretcher, and a large group of native warriors pours out of the forest and surrounds them. Kurtz speaks to them, and the natives disappear into the woods.

The manager brings Kurtz, who is quite ill, aboard the steamer. A beautiful native woman, apparently Kurtz's mistress, appears on the shore and stares out at the ship. The Russian implies that she is somehow involved with Kurtz and has caused trouble before through her influence over him. The Russian reveals to Marlow, after swearing him to secrecy, that Kurtz had ordered the attack on the steamer to make them believe he was dead in order that they might turn back and leave him to his plans. The Russian then leaves by canoe, fearing the displeasure of the manager. Kurtz disappears in the night, and Marlow goes out in search of him, finding him crawling on all fours toward the native camp. Marlow stops him and convinces him to return to the ship. They set off down the river the next morning, but Kurtz's health is failing fast.

Marlow listens to Kurtz talk while he pilots the ship, and Kurtz entrusts Marlow with a packet of personal documents, including an eloquent pamphlet on civilizing the savages which ends with a scrawled message that says, "Exterminate all the brutes!" The steamer breaks down, and they have to stop for repairs. Kurtz dies, uttering his last words—"The horror! The horror!"—in the presence of the confused Marlow. Marlow falls ill soon after and barely survives. Eventually he returns to Europe and goes to see Kurtz's Intended (his fiancée). She is still in mourning, even though it has been over a year since Kurtz's death, and she praises him as a paragon of virtue and achievement. She asks what his last words were, but Marlow cannot bring himself to shatter her illusions with the truth. Instead, he tells her that Kurtz's last word was her name.

CHARACTER LIST

Marlow   The protagonist of *Heart of Darkness*. Marlow is philosophical, independent-minded, and generally skeptical of those around him. He is also a master storyteller, eloquent and able to draw his listeners into his tale. Although Marlow shares many of his fellow Europeans' prejudices, he has seen enough of the world and has encountered enough debased white men to make him skeptical of imperialism.

Kurtz   The chief of the Inner Station and the object of Marlow's quest. Kurtz is a man of many talents—we learn, among other things, that he is a gifted musician and a fine painter—the chief of which are his charisma and his ability to lead men. Kurtz is a man who understands the power of words, and his writings are marked by an eloquence that obscures their horrifying message. Although he remains an enigma even to Marlow, Kurtz clearly exerts a powerful influence on the people in his life. His downfall seems to be a result of his willingness to ignore the hypocritical rules that govern European colonial conduct: Kurtz has "kicked himself loose of the earth" by fraternizing excessively with the natives and not keeping up appearances; in so doing, he has become wildly successful but has also incurred the wrath of his fellow white men.

General manager The chief agent of the Company in its African territory, who runs the Central Station. He owes his success to a hardy constitution that allows him to outlive all his competitors. He is average in appearance and unremarkable in abilities, but he possesses a strange capacity to produce uneasiness in those around him, keeping everyone sufficiently unsettled for him to exert his control over them.

Brickmaker The brickmaker, whom Marlow also meets at the Central Station, is a favorite of the manager and seems to be a kind of corporate spy. He never actually produces any bricks, as he is supposedly waiting for some essential element that is never delivered. He is petty and conniving and assumes that other people are too.

Chief accountant An efficient worker with an incredible habit of dressing up in spotless whites and keeping himself absolutely tidy despite the squalor and heat of the Outer Station, where he lives and works. He is one of the few colonials who seems to have accomplished anything: he has trained a native woman to care for his wardrobe.

Pilgrims The bumbling, greedy agents of the Central Station. They carry long wooden staves with them everywhere, reminding Marlow of traditional religious travelers. They all want to be appointed to a station so that they can trade for ivory and earn a commission, but none of them actually takes any effective steps toward achieving this goal. They are obsessed with keeping up a veneer of civilization and proper conduct, and are motivated entirely by self-interest. They hate the natives and treat them like animals, although in their greed and ridiculousness they appear less than human themselves.

Cannibals Natives hired as the crew of the steamer, a surprisingly reasonable and well-tempered bunch. Marlow respects their restraint and their calm acceptance of adversity. The leader of the group, in particular, seems to be intelligent and capable of ironic reflection upon his situation.

Russian trader A Russian sailor who has gone into the African interior as the trading representative of a Dutch company. He is boyish in appearance and temperament, and seems to exist wholly on the glamour of youth and the audacity of adventurousness. His brightly patched clothes remind Marlow of a harlequin. He is a devoted disciple of Kurtz's.

Helmsman   A young man from the coast trained by Marlow's predecessor to pilot the steamer. He is a serviceable pilot, although Marlow never comes to view him as much more than a mechanical part of the boat. He is killed when the steamer is attacked by natives hiding on the riverbanks.

Kurtz's African mistress   A fiercely beautiful woman loaded with jewelry who appears on the shore when Marlow's steamer arrives at and leaves the Inner Station. She seems to exert an undue influence over both Kurtz and the natives around the station, and the Russian trader points her out as someone to fear. Like Kurtz, she is an enigma: she never speaks to Marlow, and he never learns anything more about her.

Kurtz's Intended   Kurtz's naïve and long-suffering fiancée, whom Marlow goes to visit after Kurtz's death. Her unshakable certainty about Kurtz's love for her reinforces Marlow's belief that women live in a dream world, well insulated from reality.

Aunt   Marlow's doting relative, who secures him a position with the Company. She believes firmly in imperialism as a charitable activity that brings civilization and religion to suffering, simple savages. She, too, is an example for Marlow of the naïveté and illusions of women.

The men aboard the Nellie   Marlow's friends, who are with him aboard a ship on the Thames at the story's opening. They are the audience for the central story of *Heart of Darkness,* which Marlow narrates. All have been sailors at one time or another, but all now have important jobs ashore and have settled into middle-class, middle-aged lives. They represent the kind of man Marlow would have likely become had he not gone to Africa: well meaning and moral but ignorant as to a large part of the world beyond England. The narrator in particular seems to be shaken by Marlow's story. He repeatedly comments on its obscurity and Marlow's own mysterious nature.

Fresleven   Marlow's predecessor as captain of the steamer. Fresleven, by all accounts a good-tempered, nonviolent man, was killed in a dispute over some hens, apparently after striking a village chief.

ANALYSIS OF MAJOR CHARACTERS

MARLOW

Although Marlow appears in several of Conrad's other works, it is important not to view him as merely a surrogate for the author. Marlow is a complicated man who anticipates the figures of high modernism while also reflecting his Victorian predecessors. Marlow is in many ways a traditional hero: tough, honest, an independent thinker, a capable man. Yet he is also "broken" or "damaged," like T. S. Eliot's J. Alfred Prufrock or William Faulkner's Quentin Compson. The world has defeated him in some fundamental way, and he is weary, skeptical, and cynical. Marlow also mediates between the figure of the intellectual and that of the "working tough." While he is clearly intelligent, eloquent, and a natural philosopher, he is not saddled with the angst of centuries' worth of Western thought. At the same time, while he is highly skilled at what he does—he repairs and then ably pilots his own ship—he is no mere manual laborer. Work, for him, is a distraction, a concrete alternative to the posturing and excuse-making of those around him.

Marlow can also be read as an intermediary between the two extremes of Kurtz and the Company. He is moderate enough to allow the reader to identify with him, yet open-minded enough to identify at least partially with either extreme. Thus, he acts as a guide for the reader. Marlow's intermediary position can be seen in his eventual illness and recovery. Unlike those who truly confront or at least acknowledge Africa and the darkness within themselves, Marlow does not die, but unlike the Company men, who focus only on money and advancement, Marlow suffers horribly. He is thus "contaminated" by his experiences and memories, and, like Coleridge's Ancient Mariner, destined, as purgation or penance, to repeat his story to all who will listen.

KURTZ

Kurtz, like Marlow, can be situated within a larger tradition. Kurtz resembles the archetypal "evil genius": the highly gifted but ultimately degenerate individual whose fall is the stuff of legend. Kurtz is related to figures like Faustus, Satan in Milton's *Paradise Lost, Moby-Dick*'s Ahab, and *Wuthering Heights*'s Heathcliff. Like these characters, he is significant both for his style and eloquence and for his grandiose, almost megalomaniacal scheming. In a world of mundanely malicious men and "flabby devils," attracting enough attention to be worthy of damnation is indeed something. Kurtz can be criticized in the same terms that *Heart of Darkness* is sometimes criticized: style entirely overrules substance, providing a justification for amorality and evil.

In fact, it can be argued that style does not just override substance but actually masks the fact that Kurtz is utterly lacking in substance. Marlow refers to Kurtz as "hollow" more than once. This could be taken negatively, to mean that Kurtz is not worthy of contemplation. However, it also points to Kurtz's ability to function as a "choice of nightmares" for Marlow: in his essential emptiness, he becomes a cipher, a site upon which other things can be projected. This emptiness should not be read as benign, however, just as Kurtz's eloquence should not be allowed to overshadow the malice of his actions. Instead, Kurtz provides Marlow with a set of paradoxes that Marlow can use to evaluate himself and the Company's men.

Indeed, Kurtz is not so much a fully realized individual as a series of images constructed by others for their own use. As Marlow's visits with Kurtz's cousin, the Belgian journalist, and Kurtz's fiancée demonstrate, there seems to be no true Kurtz. To his cousin, he was a great musician; to the journalist, a brilliant politician and leader of men; to his fiancée, a great humanitarian and genius. All of these contrast with Marlow's version of the man, and he is left doubting the validity of his memories. Yet Kurtz, through his charisma and larger-than-life plans, remains with Marlow and with the reader.

Themes, Motifs & Symbols

Themes

Themes are the fundamental and often universal ideas explored in a literary work.

The Hypocrisy of Imperialism

Heart of Darkness explores the issues surrounding imperialism in complicated ways. As Marlow travels from the Outer Station to the Central Station and finally up the river to the Inner Station, he encounters scenes of torture, cruelty, and near-slavery. At the very least, the incidental scenery of the book offers a harsh picture of colonial enterprise. The impetus behind Marlow's adventures, too, has to do with the hypocrisy inherent in the rhetoric used to justify imperialism. The men who work for the Company describe what they do as "trade," and their treatment of native Africans is part of a benevolent project of "civilization." Kurtz, on the other hand, is open about the fact that he does not trade but rather takes ivory by force, and he describes his own treatment of the natives with the words "suppression" and "extermination": he does not hide the fact that he rules through violence and intimidation. His perverse honesty leads to his downfall, as his success threatens to expose the evil practices behind European activity in Africa.

However, for Marlow as much as for Kurtz or for the Company, Africans in this book are mostly objects: Marlow refers to his helmsman as a piece of machinery, and Kurtz's African mistress is at best a piece of statuary. It can be argued that *Heart of Darkness* participates in an oppression of nonwhites that is much more sinister and much harder to remedy than the open abuses of Kurtz or the Company's men. Africans become for Marlow a mere backdrop, a human screen against which he can play out his philosophical and existential struggles. Their existence and their exoticism enable his self-contemplation. This kind of dehumanization is harder to identify than colonial violence or open racism. While *Heart of Darkness* offers a powerful condemnation of the hypocritical operations of imperialism, it also presents a set of issues surrounding race that is ultimately more troubling.

MADNESS AS A RESULT OF IMPERIALISM

Madness is closely linked to imperialism in this book. Africa is responsible for mental disintegration as well as for physical illness. Madness has two primary functions. First, it serves as an ironic device to engage the reader's sympathies. Kurtz, Marlow is told from the beginning, is mad. However, as Marlow, and the reader, begin to form a more complete picture of Kurtz, it becomes apparent that his madness is only relative, that in the context of the Company insanity is difficult to define. Thus, both Marlow and the reader begin to sympathize with Kurtz and view the Company with suspicion. Madness also functions to establish the necessity of social fictions. Although social mores and explanatory justifications are shown throughout *Heart of Darkness* to be utterly false and even leading to evil, they are nevertheless necessary for both group harmony and individual security. Madness, in *Heart of Darkness,* is the result of being removed from one's social context and allowed to be the sole arbiter of one's own actions. Madness is thus linked not only to absolute power and a kind of moral genius but to man's fundamental fallibility: Kurtz has no authority to whom he answers but himself, and this is more than any one man can bear.

THE ABSURDITY OF EVIL

This novella is, above all, an exploration of hypocrisy, ambiguity, and moral confusion. It explodes the idea of the proverbial choice between the lesser of two evils. As the idealistic Marlow is forced to align himself with either the hypocritical and malicious colonial bureaucracy or the openly malevolent, rule-defying Kurtz, it becomes increasingly clear that to try to judge either alternative is an act of folly: how can moral standards or social values be relevant in judging evil? Is there such thing as insanity in a world that has already gone insane? The number of ridiculous situations Marlow witnesses act as reflections of the larger issue: at one station, for instance, he sees a man trying to carry water in a bucket with a large hole in it. At the Outer Station, he watches native laborers blast away at a hillside with no particular goal in mind. The absurd involves both insignificant silliness and life-or-death issues, often simultaneously. That the serious and the mundane are treated similarly suggests a profound moral confusion and a tremendous hypocrisy: it is terrifying that

Kurtz's homicidal megalomania and a leaky bucket provoke essentially the same reaction from Marlow.

MOTIFS

Motifs are recurring structures, contrasts, and literary devices that can help to develop and inform the text's major themes.

OBSERVATION AND EAVESDROPPING

Marlow gains a great deal of information by watching the world around him and by overhearing others' conversations, as when he listens from the deck of the wrecked steamer to the manager of the Central Station and his uncle discussing Kurtz and the Russian trader. This phenomenon speaks to the impossibility of direct communication between individuals: information must come as the result of chance observation and astute interpretation. Words themselves fail to capture meaning adequately, and thus they must be taken in the context of their utterance. Another good example of this is Marlow's conversation with the brickmaker, during which Marlow is able to figure out a good deal more than simply what the man has to say.

INTERIORS AND EXTERIORS

Comparisons between interiors and exteriors pervade *Heart of Darkness*. As the narrator states at the beginning of the text, Marlow is more interested in surfaces, in the surrounding aura of a thing rather than in any hidden nugget of meaning deep within the thing itself. This inverts the usual hierarchy of meaning: normally one seeks the deep message or hidden truth. The priority placed on observation demonstrates that penetrating to the interior of an idea or a person is impossible in this world. Thus, Marlow is confronted with a series of exteriors and surfaces—the river's banks, the forest walls around the station, Kurtz's broad forehead—that he must interpret. These exteriors are all the material he is given, and they provide him with perhaps a more profound source of knowledge than any falsely constructed interior "kernel."

DARKNESS

Darkness is important enough conceptually to be part of the book's title. However, it is difficult to discern exactly what it might mean, given that absolutely everything in the book is cloaked in darkness. Africa, England, and Brussels are all described as gloomy and somehow dark, even if the sun is shining brightly. Darkness thus seems to operate metaphorically and existentially rather than specifically. Darkness is the inability to see: this may sound simple, but as a description of the human condition it has profound implications. Failing to see another human being means failing to understand that individual and failing to establish any sort of sympathetic communion with him or her.

SYMBOLS

> *Symbols are objects, characters, figures, and colors used to represent abstract ideas or concepts.*

FOG

Fog is a sort of corollary to darkness. Fog not only obscures but distorts: it gives one just enough information to begin making decisions but no way to judge the accuracy of that information, which often ends up being wrong. Marlow's steamer is caught in the fog, meaning that he has no idea where he's going and no idea whether peril or open water lies ahead.

THE "WHITED SEPULCHRE"

The "whited sepulchre" is probably Brussels, where the Company's headquarters are located. A sepulchre implies death and confinement, and indeed Europe is the origin of the colonial enterprises that bring death to white men and to their colonial subjects; it is also governed by a set of reified social principles that both enable cruelty, dehumanization, and evil and prohibit change. The phrase "whited sepulchre" comes from the biblical Book of Matthew. In the passage, Matthew describes "whited sepulchres" as something beautiful on the outside but containing horrors within (the bodies of the dead); thus, the image is appropriate for Brussels, given the hypocritical Belgian rhetoric about imperialism's civilizing mission. (Belgian colonies, particularly the Congo, were notorious for the violence perpetuated against the natives.)

WOMEN

Both Kurtz's Intended and his African mistress function as blank slates upon which the values and the wealth of their respective societies can be displayed. Marlow frequently claims that women are the keepers of naïve illusions; although this sounds condemnatory, such a role is in fact crucial, as these naïve illusions are at the root of the social fictions that justify economic enterprise and colonial expansion. In return, the women are the beneficiaries of much of the resulting wealth, and they become objects upon which men can display their own success and status.

THE RIVER

The Congo River is the key to Africa for Europeans. It allows them access to the center of the continent without having to physically cross it; in other words, it allows the white man to remain always separate or outside. Africa is thus reduced to a series of two-dimensional scenes that flash by Marlow's steamer as he travels upriver. The river also seems to want to expel Europeans from Africa altogether: its current makes travel upriver slow and difficult, but the flow of water makes travel downriver, back toward "civilization," rapid and seemingly inevitable. Marlow's struggles with the river as he travels upstream toward Kurtz reflect his struggles to understand the situation in which he has found himself. The ease with which he journeys back downstream, on the other hand, mirrors his acquiescence to Kurtz and his "choice of nightmares."

SYMBOLS

SUMMARY & ANALYSIS

PART I

Beginning through Marlow's being hired as a steamboat captain.

SUMMARY

At sundown, a pleasure ship called the *Nellie* lies anchored at the mouth of the Thames, waiting for the tide to go out. Five men relax on the deck of the ship: the Director of Companies, who is also the captain and host, the Lawyer, the Accountant, Marlow, and the unnamed Narrator. The five men, old friends held together by "the bond of the sea," are restless yet meditative, as if waiting for something to happen. As darkness begins to fall, and the scene becomes "less brilliant but more profound," the men recall the great men and ships that have set forth from the Thames on voyages of trade and exploration, frequently never to return. Suddenly Marlow remarks that this very spot was once "one of the dark places of the earth." He notes that when the Romans first came to England, it was a great, savage wilderness to them. He imagines what it must have been like for a young Roman captain or soldier to come to a place so far from home and lacking in comforts.

This train of thought reminds Marlow of his sole experience as a "fresh-water sailor," when as a young man he captained a steamship going up the Congo River. He recounts that he first got the idea when, after returning from a six-year voyage through Asia, he came across a map of Africa in a London shop window, which reinvigorated his childhood fantasies about the "blank spaces" on the map.

Marlow recounts how he obtained a job with the Belgian "Company" that trades on the Congo River (the Congo was then a Belgian territory) through the influence of an aunt who had friends in the Company's administration. The Company was eager to send Marlow to Africa, because one of the Company's steamer captains had recently been killed in a scuffle with the natives.

———

ANALYSIS

Marlow's story of a voyage up the Congo River that he took as a young man is the main narrative of *Heart of Darkness*. Marlow's narrative is framed by another narrative, in which one of the listeners to Marlow's story explains the circumstances in which Marlow tells it. The narrator who begins *Heart of Darkness* is unnamed, as are the other three listeners, who are identified only by their professional occupations. Moreover, the narrator usually speaks in the first-person plural, describing what all four of Marlow's listeners think and feel. The unanimity and anonymity of Marlow's listeners combine to create the impression that they represent conventional perspectives and values of the British establishment.

For the narrator and his fellow travelers, the Thames conjures up images of famous British explorers who have set out from that river on glorious voyages. The narrator recounts the achievements of these explorers in a celebratory tone, calling them "knight-errants" of the sea, implying that such voyages served a sacred, higher purpose. The narrator's attitude is that these men promoted the glory of Great Britain, expanded knowledge of the globe, and contributed to the civilization and enlightenment of the rest of the planet.

At the time *Heart of Darkness* was written, the British Empire was at its peak, and Britain controlled colonies and dependencies all over the planet. The popular saying that "the sun never sets on the British Empire" was literally true. The main topic of *Heart of Darkness* is imperialism, a nation's policy of exerting influence over other areas through military, political, and economic coercion. The narrator expresses the mainstream belief that imperialism is a glorious and worthy enterprise. Indeed, in Conrad's time, "empire" was one of the central values of British subjects, the fundamental term through which Britain defined its identity and sense of purpose.

From the moment Marlow opens his mouth, he sets himself apart from his fellow passengers by conjuring up a past in which Britain was not the heart of civilization but the savage "end of the world." Likewise, the Thames was not the source of glorious journeys outward but the ominous beginning of a journey inward, into the heart of the wilderness. This is typical of Marlow as a storyteller: he narrates in an ironic tone, giving the impression that his audience's assumptions are wrong, but not presenting a clear alternative to those assumptions. Throughout his story, distinctions such as inward and outward, civilized and savage, dark and light, are called into question. But the irony of Marlow's story is not as pronounced as in a satire, and Marlow's and Conrad's attitudes regarding imperialism are never entirely clear.

From the way Marlow tells his story, it is clear that he is extremely critical of imperialism, but his reasons apparently have less to do with what imperialism does to colonized peoples than with what it does to Europeans. Marlow suggests, in the first place, that participation in imperial enterprises degrades Europeans by removing them from the "civilizing" context of European society, while simultaneously tempting them into violent behavior because of the hostility and lawlessness of the environment. Moreover, Marlow suggests that the mission of "civilizing" and "enlightening" native peoples is misguided, not because he believes that they have a viable civilization and culture already, but because they are so savage that the project is overwhelming and hopeless. Marlow expresses horror when he witnesses the violent maltreatment of the natives, and he argues that a kinship exists between black Africans and Europeans, but in the same breath he states that this kinship is "ugly" and horrifying, and that the kinship is extremely distant. Nevertheless, it is not a simple matter to evaluate whether Marlow's attitudes are conservative or progressive, racist or "enlightened."

In the first place, one would have to decide in relation to *whom* Marlow was conservative or progressive. Clearly, Marlow's story is shaped by the audience to whom he tells it. The anonymous narrator states that Marlow is unconventional in his ideas, and his listeners' derisive grunts and murmurs suggest that they are less inclined to question colonialism or to view Africans as human beings than he is. His criticisms of colonialism, both implicit and explicit, are pitched to an audience that is far more sympathetic toward the colonial enterprise than any twenty-first-century reader could be. The framing narrative puts a certain amount of distance between Marlow's narrative and Conrad himself. This framework suggests that the reader should regard Marlow ironically, but there are few cues within the text to suggest an alternative to Marlow's point of view.

PART I (CONTINUED)

*Marlow's visit to the Company Headquarters through his
parting with his aunt.*

SUMMARY

After he hears that he has gotten the job, Marlow travels across
the English Channel to a city that reminds him of a "whited sepulchre" (probably Brussels) to sign his employment contract at the
Company's office. First, however, he digresses to tell the story of
his predecessor with the Company, Fresleven. Much later, after the
events Marlow is about to recount, Marlow was sent to recover
Fresleven's bones, which he found lying in the center of a deserted
African village. Despite his reputation as mild mannered, Fresleven
was killed in a scuffle over some hens: after striking the village chief,
he was stabbed by the chief's son. He was left there to die, and the
superstitious natives immediately abandoned the village. Marlow
notes that he never did find out what became of the hens.

Arriving at the Company's offices, Marlow finds two sinister
women there knitting black wool, one of whom admits him to a
waiting room, where he looks at a map of Africa color-coded by
colonial powers. A secretary takes him into the inner office for a
cursory meeting with the head of the Company. Marlow signs his
contract, and the secretary takes him off to be checked over by a
doctor. The doctor takes measurements of his skull, remarking that
he unfortunately doesn't get to see those men who make it back
from Africa. More important, the doctor tells Marlow, "the changes
take place inside." The doctor is interested in learning anything that
may give Belgians an advantage in colonial situations.

With all formalities completed, Marlow stops off to say goodbye
to his aunt, who expresses her hope that he will aid in the civilization of savages during his service to the Company, "weaning those
ignorant millions from their horrid ways." Well aware that the
Company operates for profit and not for the good of humanity, and
bothered by his aunt's naïveté, Marlow takes his leave of her. Before
boarding the French steamer that is to take him to Africa, Marlow
has a brief but strange feeling about his journey: the feeling that he
is setting off for the center of the earth.

ANALYSIS

This section has several concrete objectives. The first of these is to locate Marlow more specifically within the wider history of colonialism. It is important that he goes to Africa in the service of a Belgian company rather than a British one. The map that Marlow sees in the Company offices shows the continent overlaid with blotches of color, each color standing for a different imperial power. While the map represents a relatively neutral way of describing imperial presences in Africa, Marlow's comments about the map reveal that imperial powers were not all the same. In fact, the yellow patch—"dead in the center"—covers the site of some of the most disturbing atrocities committed in the name of empire. The Belgian king, Leopold, treated the Congo as his private treasury, and the Belgians had the reputation of being far and away the most cruel and rapacious of the colonial powers. The reference to Brussels as a "whited sepulchre" is meant to bring to mind a passage from the Book of Matthew concerning hypocrisy. The Belgian monarch spoke rhetorically about the civilizing benefits of colonialism, but the Belgian version of the practice was the bloodiest and most inhumane.

This does not, however, mean that Conrad seeks to indict the Belgians and praise other colonial powers. As Marlow journeys into the Congo, he meets men from a variety of European nations, all of whom are violent and willing to do anything to make their fortunes. Moreover, it must be remembered that Marlow himself willingly goes to work for this Belgian concern: at the moment he decides to do so, his personal desire for adventure far outweighs any concerns he might have about particular colonial practices. This section of the book also introduces another set of concerns, this time regarding women. *Heart of Darkness* has been attacked by critics as misogynistic, and there is some justification for this point of view. Marlow's aunt does express a naïvely idealistic view of the Company's mission, and Marlow is thus right to fault her for being "out of touch with truth." However, he phrases his criticism so as to make it applicable to all women, suggesting that women do not even live in the same world as men and that they must be protected from reality. Moreover, the female characters in Marlow's story are extremely flat and stylized. In part this may be because Marlow uses women symbolically as representatives of "home." Marlow associates home with ideas gotten from books and religion rather than from experience. Home is the seat of naïveté, prejudice, confinement, and oppression. It is the place of people who have not gone out into the world and experienced, and who therefore cannot understand. Nonetheless, the women in Marlow's story exert a great deal of power. The influence of Marlow's aunt does not stop at getting him the job but continues to echo through the Company's correspondence in Africa. At the Company's headquarters, Marlow encounters a number of apparently influential women, hinting that all enterprises are ultimately female-driven.

Marlow's departure from the world of Belgium and women is facilitated, according to him, by two eccentric men. The first of these is Fresleven, the story of whose death serves to build suspense and suggest to the reader the transformations that Europeans undergo in Africa. By European standards, Fresleven was a good and gentle man, not one likely to die as he did. This means either that the European view of people is wrong and useless or else that there is something about Africa that makes men behave aberrantly. Both of these conclusions are difficult to accept practically or politically, and thus the story of Fresleven leaves the reader feeling ambivalent and cautious about Marlow's story to come.

The second figure presiding over Marlow's departure is the Company's doctor. The doctor is perhaps the ultimate symbol of futility: he uses external measurements to try to decipher what he admits are internal changes; moreover, his subjects either don't return from Africa or, if they do, don't return to see him. Thus his work and his advice are both totally useless. He is the first of a series of functionaries with pointless jobs that Marlow will encounter as he travels toward and then up the Congo River.

Part I (continued)

Marlow's journey down the coast of Africa through his meeting with the chief accountant.

Summary

The French steamer takes Marlow along the coast of Africa, stopping periodically to land soldiers and customshouse officers. Marlow finds his idleness vexing, and the trip seems vaguely nightmarish to him. At one point, they come across a French man-of-war shelling an apparently uninhabited forested stretch of coast. They finally arrive at the mouth of the Congo River, where Marlow boards another steamship bound for a point thirty miles upriver. The captain of the ship, a young Swede, recognizes Marlow as a seaman and invites him on the bridge. The Swede criticizes the colonial officials and tells Marlow about another Swede who recently hanged himself on his way into the interior.

Marlow disembarks at the Company's station, which is in a terrible state of disrepair. He sees piles of decaying machinery and a cliff being blasted for no apparent purpose. He also sees a group of black prisoners walking along in chains under the guard of another black man, who wears a shoddy uniform and carries a rifle. He remarks that he had already known the "devils" of violence, greed, and desire, but that in Africa he became acquainted with the "flabby, pretending, weak-eyed devil of a rapacious and pitiless folly." Finally, Marlow comes to a grove of trees and, to his horror, finds a group of dying native laborers. He offers a biscuit to one of them; seeing a bit of white European yarn tied around his neck, he wonders at its meaning. He meets a nattily dressed white man, the Company's chief accountant (not to be confused with Marlow's friend the Accountant from the opening of the book). Marlow spends ten days here waiting for a caravan to the next station. One day, the chief accountant tells him that in the interior he will undoubtedly meet Mr. Kurtz, a first-class agent who sends in as much ivory as all the others put together and is destined for advancement. He tells Marlow to let Kurtz know that everything is satisfactory at the Outer Station when he meets him. The chief accountant is afraid to send a written message for fear it will be intercepted by undesirable elements at the Central Station.

Analysis

Marlow's description of his journey on the French steamer makes use of an interior/exterior motif that continues throughout the rest of the book. Marlow frequently encounters inscrutable surfaces that tempt him to try to penetrate into the interior of situations and places. The most prominent example of this is the French man-of-war, which shells a forested wall of coastline. To Marlow's mind, the entire coastline of the African continent presents a solid green facade, and the spectacle of European guns firing blindly into that facade seems to be a futile and uncomprehending way of addressing the continent.

"The flabby, pretending, weak-eyed devil of a rapacious and pitiless folly" is one of the central images with which Marlow characterizes the behavior of the colonists. He refers back to this image at a number of key points later in the story. It is thus a very important clue as to what Marlow actually thinks is wrong about imperial-ism—Marlow's attitudes are usually implied rather than directly stated. Marlow distinguishes this devil from violence, greed, and desire, suggesting that the fundamental evil of imperialism is *not* that it perpetrates violence against native peoples, nor that it is mo-tivated by greed. The flabby, weak-eyed devil seems to be distin-guished above all by being shortsighted and foolish, unaware of what it is doing and ineffective.

The hand of the "flabby devil" is apparent in the travesties of ad-ministration and the widespread decay in the Company's stations. The colonials in the coastal station spend all their time blasting a cliff for no apparent reason, machinery lies broken all around, and supplies are poorly apportioned, resting in abundance where they are not needed and never sent to where they are needed. Given the level of waste and inefficiency, this kind of colonial activity clearly has something other than economic activity at stake, but just what that something might be is not apparent. Marlow's comments on the "flabby devil" produce a very ambivalent criticism of colonialism. Would Marlow approve of the violent exploitation and extortion of the Africans if it was done in a more clear-sighted and effective manner? This question is difficult to answer definitively.

On the other hand, Marlow is appalled by the ghastly, infernal spectacle of the grove of death, while the other colonials show no concern over it at all. For Marlow, the grove is the dark heart of the station. Marlow's horror at the grove suggests that the true evils of this colonial enterprise are dehumanization and death. All Marlow can offer these dying men are a few pieces of biscuit, and, despite the fact that Marlow is "not particularly tender," the situ-ation troubles him.

In this section, Marlow finally learns the reason for the journey he is to take up the Congo, although he does not yet realize the im-portance this reason will later take on. The chief accountant is the first to use the name of the mysterious Mr. Kurtz, speaking of him in reverent tones and alluding to a conspiracy within the Company, the particulars of which Marlow never deciphers. Again, the name "Kurtz" provides a surface that conceals a hidden and potentially threatening situation. It is appropriate, therefore, that the chief ac-countant is Marlow's informant. In his dress whites, the man epit-omizes success in the colonial world. His "accomplishment" lies in keeping up appearances, in looking as he would at home. Like everything else Marlow encounters, the chief accountant's surface may conceal a dark secret, in this case the native woman whom he has "taught"—perhaps violently and despite her "distaste for the work"—to care for his linens. Marlow has yet to find a single white man with a valid "excuse for being there" in Africa. More important, he has yet to understand why he himself is there.

PART I (CONTINUED)

Marlow's journey to the Central Station through the arrival of the Eldorado Exploring Expedition.

SUMMARY

Marlow travels overland for two hundred miles with a caravan of sixty men. He has one white companion who falls ill and must be carried by the native bearers, who start to desert because of the added burden. After fifteen days they arrive at the dilapidated Central Station. Marlow finds that the steamer he was to command has sunk. The general manager of the Central Station had taken the boat out two days before under the charge of a volunteer skipper, and they had torn the bottom out on some rocks. In light of what he later learns, Marlow suspects the damage to the steamer may have been intentional, to keep him from reaching Kurtz. Marlow soon meets with the general manager, who strikes him as an altogether average man who leads by inspiring an odd uneasiness in those around him and whose authority derives merely from his resistance to tropical disease. The manager tells Marlow that he took the boat out in a hurry to relieve the inner stations, especially the one belonging to Kurtz, who is rumored to be ill. He praises Kurtz as an exceptional agent and takes note that Kurtz is talked about on the coast.

> *The word 'ivory' rang in the air, was whispered, was sighed. You would think they were praying to it.*
> *(See* QUOTATIONS, *p. 49)*

Marlow sets to work dredging his ship out of the river and repairing it, which ends up taking three months. One day during this time, a grass shed housing some trade goods burns down, and the native laborers dance delightedly as it burns. One of the natives is accused of causing the fire and is beaten severely; he disappears into the forest after he recovers. Marlow overhears the manager talking with the brickmaker about Kurtz at the site of the burned hut. He enters into conversation with the brickmaker after the manager leaves, and ends up accompanying the man back to his quarters, which are noticeably more luxurious than those of the other agents. Marlow realizes after a while that the brickmaker is pumping him for information about the intentions of the Company's board of directors in Europe, about which, of course, Marlow knows nothing. Marlow notices an unusual painting on the wall, of a blindfolded woman with a lighted torch; when he asks about it, the brickmaker reveals that it is Kurtz's work.

The brickmaker tells Marlow that Kurtz is a prodigy, sent as a special emissary of Western ideals by the Company's directors and bound for quick advancement. He also reveals that he has seen confidential correspondence dealing with Marlow's appointment, from which he has construed that Marlow is also a favorite of the administration. They go outside, and the brickmaker tries to get himself into Marlow's good graces—and Kurtz's by proxy, since he believes Marlow is allied with Kurtz. Marlow realizes the brickmaker had planned on being assistant manager, and Kurtz's arrival has upset his chances. Seeing an opportunity to use the brickmaker's influence to his own ends, Marlow lets the man believe he really does have influence in Europe and tells him that he wants a quantity of rivets from the coast to repair his ship. The brickmaker leaves him with a veiled threat on his life, but Marlow enjoys his obvious distress and confusion.

Marlow finds his foreman sitting on the deck of the ship and tells him that they will have rivets in three weeks, and they both dance around exuberantly. The rivets do not come, however. Instead, the Eldorado Exploring Expedition, a group of white men intent on "tear[ing] treasure out of the bowels of the land," arrives, led by the manager's uncle, who spends his entire time at the station talking conspiratorially with his nephew. Marlow gives up on ever receiving the rivets he needs to repair his ship, and turns to wondering disinterestedly about Kurtz and his ideals.

ANALYSIS

As Marlow describes his caravan journey through the depopulated interior of the colony, he remarks ironically that he was becoming "scientifically interesting"—an allusion to his conversation with the company doctor in Brussels. Given this, it is curious that Marlow talks so little about the caravan journey itself. In part, this is because it's not directly relevant to his story—during this time he is neither in contact with representatives of the Company nor moving directly toward Kurtz. Nonetheless, something about this journey renders

Marlow a mystery even to himself; he starts to think of himself as a potential case study. Africa appears to him to be something that happens to a man, without his consent. One way to interpret this is that Marlow is disowning his own responsibility (and that of his fellow employees) for the atrocities committed by the Company on the natives. Because of its merciless environment and savage inhabitants, Africa itself is responsible for colonial violence. Forced to deal with his ailing companion and a group of native porters who continually desert and abandon their loads, Marlow finds himself at the top of the proverbial slippery slope.

The men he finds at the Central Station allow him to regain his perspective, however. The goings-on here are ridiculous: for example, Marlow watches a man try to extinguish a fire using a bucket with a hole in it. The manager and the brickmaker, the men in charge, are repeatedly described as hollow, "papier-mâché" figures. For Marlow, who has just experienced the surreal horrors of the continent's interior, the idea that a man's exterior may conceal only a void is disturbing. The alternative, of course, is that at the heart of these men lies not a void but a vast, malevolent conspiracy. The machinations of the manager and the brickmaker suggest that, paradoxically, both ideas are correct: that these men indeed conceal bad intentions, but that these intentions, despite the fact that they lead to apparent evil, are meaningless in light of their context. The use of religious language to describe the agents of the Central Station reinforces this paradoxical idea. Marlow calls the Company's rank and file "pilgrims," both for their habit of carrying staves (with which to beat native laborers) and for their mindless worship of the wealth to be had from ivory.

"Ivory," as it echoes through the air of the camp, sounds to Marlow like something unreal rather than a physical substance. Marlow suggests that the word echoes because the station is only a tiny "cleared speck," surrounded by an "outside" that always threatens to close in, erasing the men and their pathetic ambitions. Over and over again in this section of the book human voices are hurled against the wilderness, only to be thrown back by the river's surface or a wall of trees. No matter how evil these men are, no matter how terrible the atrocities they commit against the natives, they are insignificant in the vastness of time and the physical world. Some critics have objected to *Heart of Darkness* on the grounds that it brushes aside or makes excuses for racism and colonial violence, and that it even glamorizes them by making them the subject of Marlow's seemingly profound ruminations.

On a more concrete level, the events of this section move Marlow ever closer to the mysterious Kurtz. Kurtz increasingly appeals to Marlow as an alternative, no matter how dire, to the repellent men around him. The painting in the brickmaker's quarters, which Marlow learns is Kurtz's work, draws Marlow in: the blindfolded woman with the torch represents for him an acknowledgment of the paradox and ambiguity of the African situation, and this is a much more sophisticated response than he has seen from any of the other Europeans he has encountered. To the reader, the painting may seem somewhat heavy-handed, with its overtly allegorical depiction of blind and unseeing European attempts to bring the "light" of civilization to Africa. Marlow, however, sees in it a level of self-awareness that offers a compelling alternative to the folly he has witnessed throughout the Company.

Part II

Marlow's overhearing of the conversation between the manager and his uncle through the beginning of his voyage up the river.

Summary

One evening, as Marlow lies on the deck of his wrecked steamer, the manager and his uncle appear within earshot and discuss Kurtz. The manager complains that Kurtz has come to the Congo with plans to turn the stations into beacons of civilization and moral improvement, and that Kurtz wants to take over the manager's position. He recalls that about a year earlier Kurtz sent down a huge load of ivory of the highest quality by canoe with his clerk, but that Kurtz himself had turned back to his station after coming 300 miles down the river. The clerk, after turning over the ivory and a letter from Kurtz instructing the manager to stop sending him incompetent men, informs the manager that Kurtz has been very ill and has not completely recovered.

Continuing to converse with his uncle, the manager mentions another man whom he finds troublesome, a wandering trader. The manager's uncle tells him to go ahead and have the trader hanged, because no one will challenge his authority here. The manager's uncle also suggests that the climate may take care of all of his difficulties for him, implying that Kurtz simply may die of tropical disease. Marlow is alarmed by the apparent conspiracy between the two men and leaps to his feet, revealing himself to them. They are visibly startled but move off without acknowledging his presence. Not long after this incident, the Eldorado Expedition, led by the manager's uncle, disappears into the wilderness.

> *In a few days the Eldorado Expedition went into the patient wilderness, that closed upon it as the sea closes over a diver.*
>
> *(See* QUOTATIONS, *p. 50)*

Much later, the cryptic message arrives that all the expedition's donkeys have died. By that time, the repairs on Marlow's steamer are nearly complete, and Marlow is preparing to leave on a two-month trip up the river to Kurtz, along with the manager and several "pilgrims." The river is treacherous and the trip is difficult; the ship proceeds only with the help of a crew of natives the Europeans call cannibals, who actually prove to be quite reasonable people. The men aboard the ship hear drums at night along the riverbanks and occasionally catch glimpses of native settlements during the day, but they can only guess at what lies further inland. Marlow feels a sense of kinship between himself and the savages along the riverbanks, but his work in keeping the ship afloat and steaming keeps him safely occupied and prevents him from brooding too much.

ANALYSIS

Marlow's work ethic and professional skills are contrasted, throughout this section, with the incompetence and laziness of the Company's employees. Working to repair his ship and then piloting it up the river provides a much-needed distraction for Marlow, preventing him from brooding upon the folly of his fellow Europeans and the savagery of the natives. To Marlow's mind, work represents the fulfillment of a contract between two independent human beings. Repairing the steamer and then piloting it, he convinces himself, has little to do with the exploitation and horror he sees all around him.

Nevertheless, Marlow is continually forced to interpret the surrounding world. The description of his journey upriver is strange and disturbing. Marlow describes the trip as a journey back in time, to a "prehistoric earth." This remark reflects the European inclination to view colonized peoples as primitive, further back on the evolutionary scale than Europeans, and it recalls Marlow's comment at the beginning of his narrative about England's own past. What disturbs Marlow most about the native peoples he sees along the river, in his words, is "this suspicion of their not being inhuman": in some deep way these "savages" are like Europeans, perhaps just like the English were when Britain was colonized by Rome. Marlow's self-imposed isolation from the manager and the rest of the pilgrims forces him to consider the African members of his crew, and he is confused about what he sees. He wonders, for example, how his native fireman (the crewman who keeps the boiler going) is any different from a poorly educated, ignorant European doing the same job.

> It was unearthly, and the men were—No, they were not inhuman. Well, you know, that was the worst of it—the suspicion of their not being inhuman.
> (See QUOTATIONS, p. 51)

The mysterious figure of Kurtz is at the heart of Marlow's confusion. The manager seems to suggest that his own resistance against the consequences of the tropical climate reflects not just physical constitution but a moral fitness, or the approval of some higher power. That this could be the case is terrifying to Marlow, and in his shock he exposes his disdain of the manager to the man himself. Yet Marlow has a difficult time analyzing what he has overheard about Kurtz: if the manager's story contains any truth, then Kurtz must be a monomaniacal if not psychotic individual. Next to the petty ambitions and sycophantic maneuverings of the manager, however, Kurtz's grandiose gestures and morally ambiguous successes are appealing.

Perhaps the most remarkable aspect of this section, though, is how little actually happens. The journey up the river is full of threatened disasters, but none of them comes to pass, thanks to Marlow's skill; the most explosive potential conflict arises from an act of eavesdropping. The stillness and silence surrounding this single steamer full of Europeans in the midst of the vast African continent provoke in Marlow an attitude of restless watchfulness: he feels as if he has "no time" and must constantly "discern, mostly by inspiration, [hidden] signs." In this way, his piloting a steamboat along a treacherous river comes to symbolize his finding his way through a world of conspiracies, mysteries, and inaccessible black faces. Now that both Africa and Europe have become impenetrable to Marlow, only the larger-than-life Kurtz seems "real."

PART II (CONTINUED)

Marlow's discovery of the stack of firewood through the attack on the steamer.

SUMMARY

Fifty miles away from Kurtz's Inner Station, the steamer sights a hut with a stack of firewood and a note that says, "Wood for you. Hurry up. Approach cautiously." The signature is illegible, but it is clearly not Kurtz's. Inside the hut, Marlow finds a battered old book on seamanship with notes in the margin in what looks like code. The manager concludes that the wood must have been left by the Russian trader, a man about whom Marlow has overheard the manager complaining. After taking aboard the firewood that serves as the ship's fuel, the party continues up the river, the steamer struggling and threatening at every moment to give out completely. Marlow ponders Kurtz constantly as they crawl along toward him.

By the evening of the second day after finding the hut, they arrive at a point eight miles from Kurtz's station. Marlow wants to press on, but the manager tells him to wait for daylight, as the waters are dangerous here. The night is strangely still and silent, and dawn brings an oppressive fog. The fog lifts suddenly and then falls again just as abruptly. The men on the steamer hear a loud, desolate cry, followed by a clamor of savage voices, and then silence again. They prepare for attack. The whites are badly shaken, but the African crewmen respond with quiet alertness. The leader of the cannibals tells Marlow matter-of-factly that his people want to eat the owners of the voices in the fog. Marlow realizes that the cannibals must be terribly hungry, as they have not been allowed to go ashore to trade for supplies, and their only food, a supply of rotting hippo meat, was long since thrown overboard by the pilgrims.

The manager authorizes Marlow to take every risk in continuing on in the fog, but Marlow refuses to do so, as they will surely ground the steamer if they proceed blindly. Marlow says he does not think the natives will attack, particularly since their cries have sounded more sorrowful than warlike. After the fog lifts, at a spot a mile and a half from the station, the natives attempt to repulse the invaders. The steamer is in a narrow channel, moving along slowly next to a high bank overgrown with bushes, when suddenly the air fills with arrows. Marlow rushes inside the pilot-house. When he leans out to close the shutter on the window, he sees that the brush is swarming with natives. Suddenly, he notices a snag in the river a short way ahead of the steamer.

The pilgrims open fire with rifles from below him, and the cloud of smoke they produce obscures his sight. Marlow's African helmsman leaves the wheel to open the shutter and shoot out with a one-shot rifle, and then stands at the open window yelling at the unseen assailants on the shore. Marlow grabs the wheel and crowds the steamer close to the bank to avoid the snag. As he does so, the helmsman takes a spear in his side and falls on Marlow's feet. Marlow frightens the attackers away by sounding the steam whistle repeatedly, and they give off a prolonged cry of fear and despair. One of the pilgrims enters the pilot-house and is shocked to see the wounded helmsman. The two white men stand over him as he dies quietly. Marlow makes the repulsed and indignant pilgrim steer while he changes his shoes and socks, which are covered in the dead man's blood. Marlow expects that Kurtz is now dead as well, and he feels a terrible disappointment at the thought.

One of Marlow's listeners breaks into his narrative at this point to comment upon the absurdity of Marlow's behavior. Marlow laughs at the man, whose comfortable bourgeois existence has never brought him into contact with anything the likes of Africa. He admits that his own behavior may have been ridiculous—he did, after all, throw a pair of brand-new shoes overboard in response to the helmsman's death—but he notes that there is something legitimate about his disappointment in thinking he will never be able to meet the man behind the legend of Kurtz.

ANALYSIS

Marlow makes a major error of interpretation in this section, when he decides that the cries coming from the riverbank do not portend an attack. That he is wrong is more or less irrelevant, since the steamer has no real ability to escape. The fog that surrounds the boat is literal and metaphorical: it obscures, distorts, and leaves Marlow with only voices and words upon which to base his judgments. Indeed, this has been Marlow's situation for much of the book, as he has had to formulate a notion of Kurtz based only on secondhand accounts of the man's exploits and personality. This has been both enriching and dangerous for Marlow. On the one hand, having the figure of Kurtz available as an object for contemplation has provided a release for Marlow, a distraction from his unsavory surroundings, and Kurtz has also functioned as a kind of blank slate onto which Marlow can project his own opinions and values. Kurtz gives Marlow a sense of possibility. At the same time, Marlow's fantasizing about Kurtz has its hazards. By becoming intrigued with Kurtz, Marlow becomes dangerously alienated from, and disliked by, the Company's representatives. Moreover, Marlow focuses his energies and hopes on a man who may be nothing like the legends surrounding him. However, with nothing else to go on and no other alternatives to the manager and his ilk, Marlow has little choice.

This section contains many instances of contradictory language, reflecting Marlow's difficult and uncomfortable position. The steamer, for example, "tears slowly along" the riverbank: "to tear" usually indicates great speed or haste, but the oxymoronic addition of "slowly" immediately strips the phrase of any discernible meaning and makes it ridiculous. Marlow's companions aboard the steamer prove equally paradoxical. The "pilgrims" are rough and violent men. The "cannibals," on the other hand, conduct themselves with quiet dignity: although they are malnourished, they perform their jobs without complaint. Indeed, they even show flashes of humor, as when their leader teases Marlow by saying that they would like to eat the owners of the voices they hear coming from the shore. The combination of humane cannibals and bloodthirsty pilgrims, all overseen by a manager who manages clandestinely rather than openly, creates an atmosphere of the surreal and the absurd. Thus, it is not surprising when the ship is attacked by Stone Age weaponry (arrows and spears), and it is equally appropriate that the attack is not repelled with bullets but by manipulating the superstitions and fears of those ashore—simply by blowing the steamer's whistle. The primitive weapons used by both sides in the attack reinforce Marlow's notion that the trip up the river is a trip back in time. Marlow's response to the helmsman's death reflects the general atmosphere of contradiction and absurdity: rather than immediately mourning his right-hand man, Marlow changes his socks and shoes.

In the meantime, tension continues to build as Marlow draws nearer to Kurtz. After the attack, Marlow speculates that Kurtz may be dead, but the strange message and the book full of notes left with the firewood suggest otherwise. Marlow does not need to be told to "hurry up": his eagerness to meet Kurtz draws him onward. To meet Kurtz will be to create a coherent whole in a world sorely lacking in such things; by matching the man with his voice, Marlow hopes to come to an understanding about what happens to men in places like the Congo.

PART II (CONTINUED)

Marlow's digression about Kurtz through his meeting with the Russian trader.

SUMMARY

Marlow breaks into the narrative here to offer a digression on Kurtz. He notes that Kurtz had a fiancée, his Intended (as Kurtz called her), waiting for him in Europe. Marlow attaches no importance to Kurtz's fiancée, since, for him, women exist in an alternate fantasy world. What Marlow does find significant about Kurtz's Intended, though, is the air of possession Kurtz assumed when speaking about her: indeed, Kurtz spoke of everything—ivory, the Inner Station, the river—as being innately his. It is this sense of dark mastery that disturbs Marlow most. Marlow also mentions a report Kurtz has written at the request of the International Society for the Suppression of Savage Customs. The report is eloquent and powerful, if lacking in practical suggestions. It concludes, however, with a handwritten postscript: "Exterminate all the brutes!" Marlow suggests that this coda, the "exposition of [Kurtz's] method," is the result of Kurtz's absorption into native life—that by the time he came to write this note he had assumed a position of power with respect to the natives and had been a participant in "unspeakable rites," where sacrifices had been made in his name. At this point, Marlow also reveals that he feels he is responsible for the "care of [Kurtz's] memory," and that he has no choice but to remember and continue to talk about the man.

At the time Marlow is telling his story, he is still unsure whether Kurtz was worth the lives lost on his behalf; thus, at this point, he returns to his dead helmsman and the journey up the river. Marlow blames the helmsman's death on the man's own lack of restraint: had the helmsman not tried to fire at the men on the riverbank, he would not have been killed. Marlow drags the helmsman's body out of the pilot-house and throws it overboard. The pilgrims are indignant that the man will not receive a proper burial, and the cannibals seem to mourn the loss of a potential meal. The pilgrims have concluded Kurtz must be dead and the Inner Station destroyed, but they are cheered at the crushing defeat they believe they dealt their unseen attackers. Marlow remains skeptical and sarcastically congratulates them on the amount of smoke they have managed to produce. Suddenly, the Inner Station comes into view, somewhat decayed but still standing.

A white man, the Russian trader, beckons to them from the shore. He wears a gaudy patchwork suit and babbles incessantly. He is aware they have been attacked but tells them that everything will now be okay. The manager and the pilgrims go up the hill to retrieve Kurtz, while the Russian boards the ship to converse with Marlow. He tells Marlow that the natives mean no harm (although he is less than convincing on this point), and he confirms Marlow's theory that the ship's whistle is the best means of defense, since it will scare the natives off. He gives a brief account of himself: he has been a merchant seaman and was outfitted by a Dutch trading house to go into the African interior. Marlow gives him the book on seamanship that had been left with the firewood, and the trader is very happy to have it back. As it turns out, what Marlow had thought were encoded notes are simply notes written in Russian. The Russian trader tells Marlow that he has had trouble restraining the natives, and he suggests that the steamer was attacked because the natives do not want Kurtz to leave. The Russian also offers yet another enigmatic picture of Kurtz. According to the trader, one does not talk to Kurtz but listens to him. The trader credits Kurtz for having "enlarged his mind."

ANALYSIS

The interruption and digression at the beginning of this section suggests that Marlow has begun to feel the need to justify his own conduct. Marlow speaks of his fascination with Kurtz as something over which he has no control, as if Kurtz refuses to be forgotten. This is one of a number of instances in which Marlow suggests that a person's responsibility for his actions is not clear-cut. The Russian trader is another example of this: Marlow does not clarify whether the trader follows Kurtz because of Kurtz's charisma, or because of the trader's weakness or insanity.

Marlow repeatedly characterizes Kurtz as a voice, suggesting that eloquence is his defining trait. But Kurtz's eloquence is empty. Moreover, the picture that Marlow paints of Kurtz is extremely ironic. Both in Europe and in Africa, Kurtz is reputed to be a great humanitarian. Whereas the other employees of the Company only want to make a profit or to advance to a better position within the Company, Kurtz embodies the ideals and fine sentiments with which Europeans justified imperialism—particularly the idea that

Europeans brought light and civilization to savage peoples. But when Marlow discovers him, Kurtz has become so ruthless and rapacious that even the other managers are shocked. He refers to the ivory as his own and sets himself up as a primitive god to the natives. He has written a seventeen-page document on the suppression of savage customs, to be disseminated in Europe, but his supposed desire to "civilize" the natives is strikingly contradicted by his postscript, "Exterminate all the brutes!" Marlow is careful to tell his listeners that there was something wrong with Kurtz, some flaw in his character that made him go insane in the isolation of the Inner Station. But the obvious implication of Marlow's story is that the humanitarian ideals and sentiments justifying imperialism are empty, and are merely rationalizations for exploitation and extortion.

Marlow's behavior in the face of an increasingly insane situation demonstrates his refusal to give in to the forces of madness. By throwing the dead helmsman overboard, Marlow spares him from becoming dinner for the cannibals, but he also saves him from what the helmsman might have found even worse: the hypocrisy of a Christian burial by the pilgrims. In contrast with the pilgrims' folly and hypocrisy, Kurtz's serene dictatorship is more attractive to Marlow. In fact, as Marlow's digression at the beginning of this section suggests, right and wrong, sane and insane, are indistinguishable in this world gone mad. Force of personality is the only means by which men are judged. As Marlow's ability to captivate his listeners with his story suggests, charisma may be his link with Kurtz. What the Russian trader says of Kurtz is true of Marlow too: he is a man to whom people listen, not someone with whom they converse. Thus, the darkness in Kurtz may repel Marlow mostly because it reflects his own internal darkness.

PART III

The Russian trader's description of Kurtz through the Russian trader's departure from the Inner Station.

SUMMARY

The Russian trader begs Marlow to take Kurtz away quickly. He recounts for Marlow his initial meeting with Kurtz, telling him that Kurtz and the trader spent a night camped in the forest together, during which Kurtz discoursed on a broad range of topics. The trader again asserts that listening to Kurtz has greatly enlarged his mind. His connection to Kurtz, however, has gone through periods of rise and decline. He nursed Kurtz through two illnesses but sometimes would not see him for long periods of time, during which Kurtz was out raiding the countryside for ivory with a native tribe he had gotten to follow him. Although Kurtz has behaved erratically and once even threatened to shoot the trader over a small stash of ivory, the trader nevertheless insists that Kurtz cannot be judged as one would judge a normal man. He has tried to get Kurtz to return to civilization several times. The Russian tells Marlow that Kurtz is extremely ill now. As he listens to the trader, Marlow idly looks through his binoculars and sees that what he had originally taken for ornamental balls on the tops of fence posts in the station compound are actually severed heads turned to face the station house. He is repelled but not particularly surprised. The Russian apologetically explains that these are the heads of rebels, an explanation that makes Marlow laugh out loud. The Russian makes a point of telling Marlow that he has had no medicine or supplies with which to treat Kurtz; he also asserts that Kurtz has been shamefully abandoned by the Company.

At that moment, the pilgrims emerge from the station-house with Kurtz on an improvised stretcher, and a group of natives rushes out of the forest with a piercing cry. Kurtz speaks to the natives, and the natives withdraw and allow the party to pass. The manager and the pilgrims lay Kurtz in one of the ship's cabins and give him his mail, which they have brought from the Central Station. Someone has written to Kurtz about Marlow, and Kurtz tells him that he is "glad" to see him. The manager enters the cabin to speak with Kurtz, and Marlow withdraws to the steamer's deck. From here he sees two natives standing near the river with impressive headdresses and spears, and a beautiful native woman draped in ornaments pacing gracefully along the shore. She stops and stares out at the steamer for a while and then moves away into the forest. Marlow notes that she must be wearing several elephant tusks' worth of ornaments. The Russian implies that she is Kurtz's mistress, and states that she has caused him trouble through her influence over Kurtz. He adds that he would have tried to shoot her if she had tried to come aboard. The trader's comments are interrupted by the sound of Kurtz yelling at the manager inside the cabin. Kurtz accuses the men of coming for the ivory rather than to help him, and he threatens the manager for interfering with his plans.

The manager comes out and takes Marlow aside, telling him that they have done everything possible for Kurtz, but that his unsound methods have closed the district off to the Company for the time being. He says he plans on reporting Kurtz's "complete want of judgment" to the Company's directors. Thoroughly disgusted by the manager's hypocritical condemnation of Kurtz, Marlow tells the manager that he thinks Kurtz is a "remarkable man." With this statement, Marlow permanently alienates himself from the manager and the rest of the Company functionaries. Like Kurtz, Marlow is now classified among the "unsound." As the manager walks off, the Russian approaches again, to confide in Marlow that Kurtz ordered the attack on the steamer, hoping that the manager would assume he was dead and turn back. After the Russian asks Marlow to protect Kurtz's reputation, Marlow tells the Russian that the manager has spoken of having the Russian hanged. The trader is not surprised and, after hitting Marlow up for tobacco, gun cartridges, and shoes, leaves in a canoe with some native paddlers.

ANALYSIS

Until this point, Marlow's narrative has featured prominently mysterious signs and symbols, which Marlow has struggled to interpret. Now he confronts the reality of the Inner Station, and witnesses that symbols possess a disturbing power to define "reality" and influence people. The natives perceive Kurtz as a mythical deity and think that the guns carried by his followers are lightning bolts, symbols of power rather than actual weapons. Marlow and the Russian trader are aware of the guns' power to kill, however, and they react nervously at Kurtz's show of force. Kurtz himself acts as a symbol for all of the other characters, not only the natives. To the Russian trader, he is a source of knowledge about everything from economics to love. To Marlow, Kurtz offers "a choice of nightmares," something distinct from the hypocritical evils of the manager. To the manager and the pilgrims, he is a scapegoat, someone they can punish for failing to uphold the "civilized" ideals of colonialism, thereby making themselves seem less reprehensible. The long-awaited appearance of the man himself demonstrates just how empty these formulations are, however. He is little more than a skeleton, and even his name proves not to be an adequate description of him (Kurtz means "short" in German, but Kurtz is tall). Thus, both words and symbols are shown to have little basis in reality.

Kurtz's African mistress provides another example of the power of symbols and the dubious value of words. The woman is never given the title "mistress," although it seems clear that she and Kurtz have a sexual relationship. To acknowledge through the use of the term that a white man and a black woman could be lovers seems to be more than the manager and the Russian trader are willing to do. Despite their desire to discredit Kurtz, the transgression implied by Kurtz's relationship is not something they want to discuss. To Marlow, the woman is above all an aesthetic and economic object. She is "superb" and "magnificent," dripping with the trappings of wealth. As we have seen in earlier sections of Marlow's narrative, he believes that women represent the ideals of a civilization: it is on their behalf that men undertake economic enterprises, and it is their beauty that comes to symbolize nations and ways of life. Thus, Kurtz's African mistress plays a role strikingly like that of Kurtz's fiancée: like his fiancée, Kurtz's mistress is lavished with material goods, both to keep her in her place and to display his success and wealth.

Marlow and the Russian trader offer alternate perspectives throughout this section. The Russian is naive to the point of idiocy, yet he has much in common with Marlow. Both have come to Africa in search of something experiential, and both end up aligning themselves with Kurtz against other Europeans. The Russian, who seems to exist upon "glamour" and youth, is drawn to the systematic qualities of Kurtz's thought. Although Kurtz behaves irrationally toward him, for the trader, the great man's philosophical mind offers a bulwark against the even greater irrationality of Africa. For Marlow, on the other hand, Kurtz represents the choice of outright perversion over hypocritical justifications of cruelty. Marlow and the Russian are disturbingly similar to one another, as the transfer of responsibility for Kurtz's "reputation" from the Russian to Marlow suggests. The manager's implicit condemnation of Marlow as "unsound" is correct, if for the wrong reasons: by choosing Kurtz, Marlow has, in fact, like the cheerfully idiotic Russian, merely chosen one kind of nightmare over another.

PART III (CONTINUED)

Marlow's nighttime pursuit of Kurtz through the steamship's departure from the Inner Station.

SUMMARY

Remembering the Russian trader's warning, Marlow gets up in the middle of the night and goes out to look around for any sign of trouble. From the deck of the steamer, he sees one of the pilgrims with a group of the cannibals keeping guard over the ivory, and he sees the fires of the natives' camp in the forest. He hears a drum and a steady chanting, which lulls him into a brief sleep. A sudden outburst of yells wakes him, but the loud noise immediately subsides into a rhythmic chanting once again. Marlow glances into Kurtz's cabin only to find that Kurtz is gone. He is unnerved, but he does not raise an alarm, and instead decides to leave the ship to search for Kurtz himself.

He finds a trail in the grass and realizes that Kurtz must be crawling on all fours. Marlow runs along the trail after him; Kurtz hears him coming and rises to his feet. They are now close to the fires of the native camp, and Marlow realizes the danger of his situation, as Kurtz could easily call out to the natives and have him killed. Kurtz tells him to go away and hide, and Marlow looks over and sees the imposing figure of a native sorcerer silhouetted against the fire. Marlow asks Kurtz if he knows what he is doing, and Kurtz replies emphatically that he does. Despite his physical advantage over the invalid, Marlow feels impotent, and threatens to strangle Kurtz if he should call out to the natives. Kurtz bemoans the failure of his grand schemes, and Marlow reassures him that he is thought a success in Europe. Sensing the other man's vulnerability, Marlow tells Kurtz he will be lost if he continues on. Kurtz's resolution falters, and Marlow helps him back to the ship.

The steamer departs the next day at noon, and the natives appear on the shore to watch it go. Three men painted with red earth and wearing horned headdresses wave charms and shout incantations at the ship as it steams away. Marlow places Kurtz in the pilot-house to get some air, and Kurtz watches through the open window as his mistress rushes down to the shore and calls out to him. The crowd responds to her cry with an uproar of its own. Marlow sounds the whistle as he sees the pilgrims get out their rifles, and the crowd scatters, to the pilgrims' dismay. Only the woman remains standing on the shore as the pilgrims open fire, and Marlow's view is obscured by smoke.

ANALYSIS

Marlow describes his developing relationship with Kurtz in terms of intimacy and betrayal. The extravagant symbolism of the previous section is largely absent here. Instead, Marlow and Kurtz confront one another in a dark forest, with no one else around. Marlow seems to stand both physically and metaphorically between Kurtz and a final plunge into madness and depravity, as symbolized by the native sorcerer presiding over the fire at the native camp. It occurs to Marlow that, from a practical standpoint, he should strangle Kurtz. The nearness of the natives puts Marlow in danger, and Kurtz is going to die soon anyway. Yet to kill Kurtz would not only be hypocritical but, for Marlow, impossible. As Marlow perceives it, Kurtz's "crime" is that he has rejected all of the principles and obligations that make up European society. Marlow "could not appeal [to him] in the name of anything high or low." Kurtz has become an entirely self-sufficient unit, a man who has "kicked himself loose of the earth." In a way, the Russian trader is right to claim that Kurtz cannot be judged by normal standards. Kurtz has already judged, and rejected, the standards by which other people are judged, and thus it seems irrelevant to bring such standards back to bear on him.

Marlow suggests that Africa is responsible for Kurtz's current condition. Having rejected European society, Kurtz has been forced to look into his own soul, and this introspection has driven him mad. Kurtz's illness, resulting from his body's inability to function outside of a normal (i.e., European) environment, reflects his psyche's inability to function outside of a normal social environment. Despite the hypocrisy latent in social norms, these norms provide a framework of security and defined expectations within which an individual can exist. In Freudian terms, we might say that Kurtz has lost his superego, and that it is the terror of limitless freedom, with no oversight or punishment, that leads to his madness. Kurtz now knows himself to be capable of anything. Marlow claims that his recognition of this capacity forces him to look into Kurtz's soul, and that his coming face-to-face with Kurtz is his "punishment." Marlow's epiphany about the roots of Kurtz's madness does lead to a moment of profound intimacy between the two men, as Marlow both comes to understand Kurtz's deepest self-awareness and in turn is forced to apply this realization to himself, as he sees that

Kurtz's actual depravity mirrors his own potential depravity. Given this, for Marlow to betray Kurtz—whether by killing him or by siding with the manager against him—would be to betray himself. Later in the narrative, when Marlow speaks of his "choice of nightmares," the alternatives of which he speaks are social injustice and cruelty on the one hand, and the realization that one's soul is empty and infinitely capable of depravity on the other hand.

The pilgrims' fervent desire to use the natives for target practice as the steamer departs clearly reflects the former choice. Kurtz's mistress and, more generally, his level of control over the natives at the station are reminders that the kind of self-immolation that Kurtz has chosen has nothing inherently noble about it. Kurtz's realization of his potential for depravity has not kept him from exercising it. Significantly, Kurtz's mistress demonstrates that although Kurtz has "kicked himself loose from the earth," he cannot help but reenact some of the social practices he has rejected. There is something sentimental about her behavior, despite her hard-edged appearance, and her relationship with Kurtz seems to have some of the same characteristics of romance, manipulation, and adoration as a traditional European male-female coupling. Moreover, as was noted in the previous section, with all her finery she has come to symbolize value and economic enterprise, much as a European woman would. Critics have often read her as a racist and misogynist stereotype, and in many ways this is true. However, the fact that Kurtz and Marlow both view her as a symbol rather than as a person is part of the point: we are supposed to recognize that she is actively stereotyped by Kurtz and by Marlow.

PART III (CONTINUED)

Marlow's journey back down the river through his falling ill.

SUMMARY

The current speeds the steamer's progress back toward civilization. The manager, certain that Kurtz will soon be dead, is pleased to have things in hand; he condescendingly ignores Marlow, who is now clearly of the "unsound" but harmless party. The pilgrims are disdainful, and Marlow, for the most part, is left alone with Kurtz. As he had done with the Russian trader, Kurtz takes advantage of his captive audience to hold forth on a variety of subjects. Marlow is alternately impressed and disappointed. Kurtz's philosophical musings are interspersed with grandiose and childish plans for fame and fortune.

> *The brown current ran swiftly out of the heart of*
> *darkness, bearing us down towards the sea with twice*
> *the speed of our upward progress; and Kurtz's life was*
> *running swiftly, too. . . .*
>
> (See QUOTATIONS, p. 52)

The steamer breaks down, and repairs take some time. Marlow is slowly becoming ill, and the work is hard on him. Kurtz seems troubled, probably because the delay has made him realize that he probably will not make it back to Europe alive. Worried that the manager will gain control of his "legacy," Kurtz gives Marlow a bundle of papers for safekeeping. Kurtz's ramblings become more abstract and more rhetorical as his condition worsens. Marlow believes he is reciting portions of articles he has written for the newspapers: Kurtz thinks it his "duty" to disseminate his ideas. Finally, one night, Kurtz admits to Marlow that he is "waiting for death." As Marlow approaches, Kurtz seems to be receiving some profound knowledge or vision, and the look on his face forces Marlow to stop and stare. Kurtz cries out—"The horror! The horror!"—and Marlow flees, not wanting to watch the man die. He joins the manager in the dining hall, which is suddenly overrun by flies. A moment later, a servant comes in to tell them, "Mistah Kurtz—he dead."

The pilgrims bury Kurtz the next day. Marlow succumbs to illness and nearly dies himself. He suffers greatly, but the worst thing about his near-death experience is his realization that in the end he would have "nothing to say." Kurtz, he realizes, was remarkable because he "had something to say. He said it." Marlow remembers little about the time of his illness. Once he has recovered sufficiently, he leaves Africa and returns to Brussels.

ANALYSIS

Both Kurtz and Marlow experience a brief interlude during which they float between life and death, although their final fates differ. For Kurtz, the imminence of death ironically causes him to seek to return to the world from which he had "kicked himself loose." Suddenly, his legacy and his ideas seem very important to him, and he turns to Marlow to preserve them. Kurtz's final ambitions—to be famous and feted by kings, to have his words read by millions—

suggest a desire to change the world. This is a change from his previous formulations, which posited a choice between acquiescence to existing norms or total isolation from society. However, these final schemes of Kurtz's (which Marlow describes as "childish") reflect Kurtz's desire for self-aggrandizement rather than any progressive social program. Kurtz dies. His last words are paradoxically full of meaning yet totally empty. It is possible to read them as an acknowledgment of Kurtz's own misguided life and despicable acts, as a description of his inner darkness; certainly, to do so is not inappropriate. However, it is important to note both their eloquence and their vagueness. True to form, Kurtz dies in a spasm of eloquence. His last words are poetic and profound, delivered in his remarkable voice. However, they are so nonspecific that they defy interpretation. The best one can do is to guess at their meaning.

> *I was within a hair's-breadth of the last opportunity*
> *for pronouncement, and I found with humiliation that*
> *probably I would have nothing to say.*
> (See QUOTATIONS, *p. 53)*

Does this mean that Marlow is wrong, that Kurtz has "nothing," not "something to say"? Kurtz's last words could refer to the terrible nothingness at the heart of his soul and his ideas, the ultimate failure of his "destiny." In a way this is true: Kurtz's agony seems to be a response to a generalized lack of substance. In his dying words as in his life, though, Kurtz creates an enigma, an object for contemplation, which certainly is something. His legacy, in fact, would seem to be Marlow, who, like the Russian trader, seems to have had his mind "enlarged" by Kurtz. Marlow, though, finds that he himself has "nothing" to say, and thus Kurtz's life and his dying words oscillate between absolute emptiness and an overabundance of meaning. The "horror" is either nothing or everything, but it is not simply "something."

The actual moment of Kurtz's death is narrated indirectly. First, Kurtz's words—"The horror! The horror!"—anticipate and mark its beginning. Then flies, the symbol of slow, mundane decay and disintegration (as opposed to catastrophic or dramatic destruction), swarm throughout the ship, as if to mark the actual moment. Finally, the servant arrives to bring the moment to its close with his surly, unpoetic words. The roughness of "Mistah Kurtz—he dead" contrasts with Kurtz's self-generated epitaph, again bringing a blunt reality (death) into conflict with a subjective state (horror). It is interesting to consider why T. S. Eliot might have chosen the servant's line as the epigraph to his poem "The Hollow Men." The impenetrability of the brief moment of Kurtz's death and his reduction to something "buried in a muddy hole" indicate the final impossibility of describing either Kurtz or his ideas.

Kurtz's death is very nearly followed by Marlow's demise. Although both men's illnesses are blamed on climate, it seems as if they are both also the result of existential crisis. Furthermore, an element of metaphorical contagion seems to be involved, as Kurtz transmits both his memory and his poor health to Marlow. Unlike Kurtz, though, Marlow recovers. Having "nothing to say" seems to save him. He does not slip into the deadly paradox of wanting to be both free of society and an influence on it, and he will not have to sacrifice himself for his ideas. For Marlow, guarding Kurtz's legacy is not inconsistent with isolation from society. Remaining loyal to Kurtz is best done by remaining true to his experience, and by not offering up his story to those who will misinterpret or fail to understand it. Marlow keeps these principles in mind once he arrives in Brussels. His reasons for telling this story to his audience aboard the *Nellie* are more difficult to discern.

PART III (CONTINUED)

Marlow's return to Brussels through the conclusion.

SUMMARY

Marlow barely survives his illness. Eventually he returns to the "sepulchral city," Brussels. He resents the people there for their petty self-importance and smug complacency. His aunt nurses him back to health, but his disorder is more emotional than physical. A bespectacled representative of the Company comes to retrieve the packet of papers Kurtz entrusted to Marlow, but Marlow will give him only the pamphlet on the "Suppression of Savage Customs," with the postscript (the handwritten "Exterminate all the brutes!") torn off. The man threatens legal action to obtain the rest of the packet's contents. Another man, calling himself Kurtz's cousin, appears and takes some letters to the family. The cousin tells him that Kurtz had been a great musician, although he does not elaborate further. Marlow and the cousin ponder Kurtz's myriad talents and decide that he is best described as a "universal genius." A journalist colleague of Kurtz's appears and takes the pamphlet for publication. This man believes Kurtz's true skills were in popular or extremist politics.

Finally, Marlow is left with only a few letters and a picture of Kurtz's Intended. Marlow goes to see her without really knowing why. Kurtz's memory comes flooding back to him as he stands on her doorstep. He finds the Intended still in mourning, though it has been over a year since Kurtz's death. He gives her the packet, and she asks if he knew Kurtz well. He replies that he knew him as well as it is possible for one man to know another.

His presence fulfills her need for a sympathetic ear, and she continually praises Kurtz. Her sentimentality begins to anger Marlow, but he holds back his annoyance until it gives way to pity. She says she will mourn Kurtz forever, and asks Marlow to repeat his last words to give her something upon which to sustain herself. Marlow lies and tells her that Kurtz's last word was her name. She responds that she was certain that this was the case. Marlow ends his story here, and the narrator looks off into the dark sky, which makes the waterway seem "to lead into the heart of an immense darkness."

ANALYSIS

Marlow's series of encounters with persons from Kurtz's former life makes him question the value he places on his memories of Kurtz. Kurtz's cousin and the journalist both offer a version of Kurtz that seems not to resemble the man Marlow knew. Kurtz, in fact, seems to have been all things to all people—someone who has changed their life and now serves as a kind of symbolic figure presiding over their existence. This makes Marlow's own experience of Kurtz less unique and thus perhaps less meaningful. The fact that he shares Kurtz with all of these overconfident, self-important people, most of whom will never leave Brussels, causes Kurtz to seem common, and less profound. In reality, Marlow's stream of visitors do not raise any new issues: in their excessive praise of Kurtz and their own lack of perspective, they resemble the Russian trader, who also took Kurtz as a kind of guru.

Marlow goes to see Kurtz's Intended in a state of profound uncertainty. He is unsure whether his version of Kurtz has any value either as a reflection of reality or as a philosophical construct. In response to the woman's simple question as to whether he knew Kurtz well, he can only reply that he knew him "'as well as it is possible for one man to know another.'" Given what the preceding narrative has shown about the possibilities for "knowing" another person in any meaningful sense, the reader can easily see that Marlow's reply to Kurtz's Intended is a qualification, not an affirmation: Marlow barely knows himself. By the end of Marlow's visit with the woman, the reader is also aware, even if Marlow is not, that the kinds of illusions and untruths which Marlow accuses women of perpetuating are in fact not dissimilar from those fictions men use to understand their own experiences and justify such things as colonialism. Marlow has much more in common with Kurtz's Intended than he would like to admit.

Kurtz's Intended, like Marlow's aunt and Kurtz's mistress, is a problematic female figure. Marlow praises her for her "mature capacity for fidelity, for belief, for suffering," suggesting that the most valuable traits in a woman are passive. Conrad's portrayal of the Intended has thus been criticized for having misogynist overtones, and there is some justification for this point of view. She is a repository of conservative ideas about what it means to be white and European, upholding fine-sounding but ultimately useless notions of heroism and romance.

Although both Marlow and the Intended construct idealized versions of Kurtz to make sense out of their respective worlds, in the end, Marlow's version of Kurtz is upheld as the more profound one. Marlow emphasizes his disgust at the complacency of the people he meets in Brussels in order to validate his own store of worldly experience. Marlow's narrative implies that his version of Kurtz, as well as his accounts of Africa and imperialism, are inherently better and truer than other people's because of what he has experienced. This notion is based on traditional ideas of heroism, involving quests and trials in the pursuit of knowledge. In fact, by seeming to legitimize activities like imperialism for their experiential value for white men—in other words, by making it appear that Africa is the key to philosophical truth—the ending of *Heart of Darkness* introduces a much greater horror than any Marlow has encountered in the Congo. Are the evils of colonialism excusable in the name of "truth" or knowledge, even if they are not justifiable in the name of wealth? This paradox accounts at least partially for the novella's frame story. Marlow recounts his experiences to his friends because doing so establishes an implicit comparison. The other men aboard the *Nellie* are the kind of men who benefit economically from imperialism, while Marlow has benefited mainly experientially. While Marlow's "truth" may be more profound than that of his friends or Kurtz's Intended, it may not justify the cost of its own acquisition.

IMPORTANT QUOTATIONS EXPLAINED

1. "The word 'ivory' rang in the air, was whispered, was
    sighed. You would think they were praying to it. A taint
    of imbecile rapacity blew through it all, like a whiff from
    some corpse. By Jove! I've never seen anything so unreal in
    my life. And outside, the silent wilderness surrounding this
    cleared speck on the earth struck me as something great
    and invincible, like evil or truth, waiting patiently for the
    passing away of this fantastic invasion."

This quote, from the fourth section of Part I, offers Marlow's initial
impression of the Central Station. The word "ivory" has taken on
a life of its own for the men who work for the Company. To them,
it is far more than the tusk of an elephant; it represents economic
freedom, social advancement, an escape from a life of being an em-
ployee. The word has lost all connection to any physical reality and
has itself become an object of worship. Marlow's reference to a decaying corpse is both literal and figurative: elephants and native Africans both die as a result of the white man's pursuit of ivory, and the
entire enterprise is rotten at the core. The cruelties and the greed are
both part of a greater, timeless evil, yet they are petty in the scheme
of the greater order of the natural world.

2. "In a few days the Eldorado Expedition went into the patient wilderness, that closed upon it as the sea closes over a diver. Long afterwards the news came that all the donkeys were dead. I know nothing as to the fate of the less valuable animals. They, no doubt, like the rest of us, found what they deserved. I did not inquire."

During the first section of Part II, Marlow watches the Eldorado Exploring Expedition, a band of freelance bandits, reequip and then depart from the Central Station. This enigmatic report is the only news he receives concerning their fate. The dry irony of this quote is characteristic of Marlow, who by this point has truly come to see white men as the "less valuable animals." Although he chalks up the Expedition's fate to some idea of destiny or just reward, Marlow has already come to distrust such moral formulations: this is why he does not seek further information about the Expedition. Again he mentions a "patient wilderness": the Expedition's fate is insignificant in the face of larger catastrophes and even less meaningful when considered in the scope of nature's time frame.

3.   "It was unearthly, and the men were—No, they were not
        inhuman. Well, you know, that was the worst of it—the
        suspicion of their not being inhuman. It would come
        slowly to one. They howled and leaped, and spun, and
        made horrid faces; but what thrilled you was just the
        thought of their humanity—like yours—the thought of
        your remote kinship with this wild and passionate uproar.
        Ugly. Yes, it was ugly enough; but if you were man enough
        you would admit to yourself that there was in you just the
        faintest trace of a response to the terrible frankness of that
        noise, a dim suspicion of there being a meaning in it which
        you—you so remote from the night of first ages—could
        comprehend. And why not?"

As Marlow journeys up the river toward the Inner Station in the
first section of Part II, he catches occasional glimpses of native vil-
lages along the riverbanks. More often, though, he simply hears
things: drums, chants, howls. These engage his imagination, and
the fact that they do so troubles him, because it suggests, as he
says, a "kinship" with these men, whom he has so far been able to
classify as "inhuman." This moment is one of several in the text
in which Marlow seems to admit the limits of his own perception.
These moments allow for a reading of *Heart of Darkness* that is
much more critical of colonialism and much more ironic about the
stereotypes it engenders. Nevertheless, it is important to notice that
Marlow still casts Africans as a primitive version of himself rather
than as potential equals.

QUOTATIONS

4.   "The brown current ran swiftly out of the heart of
      darkness, bearing us down towards the sea with twice the
      speed of our upward progress; and Kurtz's life was running
      swiftly, too, ebbing, ebbing out of his heart into the sea of
      inexorable time. . . . I saw the time approaching when I
      would be left alone of the party of 'unsound method.'"

This quote, which comes as the steamer begins its voyage back from
the Inner Station in the third section of Part III, with Kurtz and
his ivory aboard, brings together the images of the river and the
"heart of darkness" which it penetrates. The river is something that
separates Marlow from the African interior: while on the river he is
exterior to, even if completely surrounded by, the jungle. Furthermore, despite its "brown current," the river inexorably brings him
back to white civilization. The first sentence of this quote suggests
that Marlow and Kurtz have been able to leave the "heart of darkness" behind, but Kurtz's life seems to be receding along with the
"darkness," and Marlow, too, has been permanently scarred by it,
since he is now ineradicably marked as being of Kurtz's party. Thus,
it seems that the "darkness" is in fact internalized, that it is part of
some fundamental if ironic "unsoundness."

5.   "I was within a hair's-breadth of the last opportunity
      for pronouncement, and I found with humiliation that
      probably I would have nothing to say. This is the reason
      why I affirm that Kurtz was a remarkable man. He had
      something to say. He said it. . . . He had summed up—he
      had judged. 'The horror!' He was a remarkable man."

At the beginning of the final section of Part III, Marlow has just recovered from his near-fatal illness. His "nothing to say" is not reflective of a lack of substance but rather of his realization that anything he might have to say would be so ambiguous and so profound as to be impossible to put into words. Kurtz, on the other hand, is "remarkable" for his ability to cut through ambiguity, to create a definite "something." Paradoxically, though, the final formulation of that "something" is so vague as to approach "nothing": "'The horror!'" could be almost anything. However, perhaps Kurtz is most fascinating to Marlow because he has had the courage to judge, to deny ambiguity. Marlow is aware of Kurtz's intelligence and the man's appreciation of paradox, so he also knows that Kurtz's rabid systematization of the world around him has been an act and a lie. Yet Kurtz, on the strength of his hubris and his charisma, has created out of himself a way of organizing the world that contradicts generally accepted social models. Most important, he has created an impressive legacy: Marlow will ponder Kurtz's words ("'The horror!'") and Kurtz's memory for the rest of his life. By turning himself into an enigma, Kurtz has done the ultimate: he has ensured his own immortality.

QUOTATIONS

Key Facts

FULL TITLE
Heart of Darkness

AUTHOR
Joseph Conrad

TYPE OF WORK
Novella (between a novel and a short story in length and scope)

GENRE
Symbolism, colonial literature, adventure tale, frame story, almost a romance in its insistence on heroism and the supernatural and its preference for the symbolic over the realistic

LANGUAGE
English

TIME AND PLACE WRITTEN
England, 1898–1899; inspired by Conrad's journey to the Congo in 1890

DATE OF FIRST PUBLICATION
Serialized in *Blackwood's* magazine in 1899; published in 1902 in the volume *Youth: A Narrative; and Two Other Stories*

PUBLISHER
J. M. Dent & Sons, Ltd.

NARRATOR
There are two narrators: an anonymous passenger on a pleasure ship, who listens to Marlow's story, and Marlow himself, a middle-aged ship's captain.

POINT OF VIEW
The first narrator speaks in the first-person plural, on behalf of four other passengers who listen to Marlow's tale. Marlow narrates his story in the first person, describing only what he witnessed and experienced, and providing his own commentary on the story.

TONE

Ambivalent: Marlow is disgusted at the brutality of the Company and horrified by Kurtz's degeneration, but he claims that any thinking man would be tempted into similar behavior.

TENSE

Past

SETTING (TIME)

Latter part of the nineteenth century, probably sometime between 1876 and 1892

SETTING (PLACE)

Opens on the Thames River outside London, where Marlow is telling the story that makes up *Heart of Darkness*. Events of the story take place in Brussels, at the Company's offices, and in the Congo, then a Belgian territory.

PROTAGONIST

Marlow

MAJOR CONFLICT

Both Marlow and Kurtz confront a conflict between their images of themselves as "civilized" Europeans and the temptation to abandon morality completely once they leave the context of European society.

RISING ACTION

The brutality Marlow witnesses in the Company's employees, the rumors he hears that Kurtz is a remarkable and humane man, and the numerous examples of Europeans breaking down mentally or physically in the environment of Africa.

CLIMAX

Marlow's discovery, upon reaching the Inner Station, that Kurtz has completely abandoned European morals and norms of behavior

FALLING ACTION

Marlow's acceptance of responsibility for Kurtz's legacy, Marlow's encounters with Company officials and Kurtz's family and friends, Marlow's visit to Kurtz's Intended

KEY FACTS

THEMES

The hypocrisy of imperialism, madness as a result of imperialism, the absurdity of evil

MOTIFS

Darkness (very seldom opposed by light), interiors vs. surfaces (kernel/shell, coast/inland, station/forest, etc.), ironic understatement, hyperbolic language, inability to find words to describe situation adequately, images of ridiculous waste, upriver versus downriver/toward and away from Kurtz/away from and back toward civilization (quest or journey structure)

SYMBOLS

Rivers, fog, women (Kurtz's Intended, his African mistress), French warship shelling forested coast, grove of death, severed heads on fence posts, Kurtz's "Report," dead helmsman, maps, "whited sepulchre" of Brussels, knitting women in Company offices, man trying to fill bucket with hole in it

FORESHADOWING

Permeates every moment of the narrative—mostly operates on the level of imagery, which is consistently dark, gloomy, and threatening

STUDY QUESTIONS

1. *The Nigerian writer Chinua Achebe has claimed that* Heart of Darkness *is an "offensive and deplorable book" that "set[s] Africa up as a foil to Europe, as a place of negations at once remote and vaguely familiar, in comparison with which Europe's own state of spiritual grace will be manifest." Achebe says that Conrad does not provide enough of an outside frame of reference to enable the novel to be read as ironic or critical of imperialism. Based on the evidence in the text, argue for or against Achebe's assertion.*

This novel opens with Marlow noting that England was once one of the dark places of the earth. This can be read two ways. First, Marlow may mean that "Western" civilization is just as barbarous as African civilizations. This reading may contradict the European belief that white men are more "civilized" than their colonial subjects, but it hardly mitigates racist notions about primitive or degraded "savages": it just means that Europeans are as "bad" as that which they have constructed as the lowest form of humanity. The second way to read Marlow's comment is as a reference to the historical precedent for colonization of other peoples. England, after all, was once a Roman colony. Again, this reading is more ambiguous than it seems. On the one hand, it implies that all peoples need a more advanced civilization to come along and save them; on the other hand, though, it also implies that the British would and did react to an exploitative colonial presence in the same way the Africans are reacting. The ambiguity and angst inherent in the statements this book makes about imperialism suggest that Achebe's condemnation is too simple. Additionally, moments of irony and narrative unreliability are scattered throughout the text, suggesting that Conrad does indeed provide a framework against which *Heart of Darkness* can be read as critical or ironic. At the same time, the fact that Africa is set up as a place where white men can go to have profound experiences and think philosophically could be read as reinforcing Achebe's claim that "Africa [is used] as [a] setting and backdrop which eliminates the African as human factor" in a troubling way.

2.   *Discuss the importance of the Congo River in this
      narrative. Why does Marlow travel primarily by boat
      and seldom on land?*

The river is a space that allows Marlow to be simultaneously within
and removed from the African interior. On the river he is isolated, a
spectator. To discern his surroundings, he must watch and interpret
the thin margin of land at the river's edge: from this he must guess
at what lies behind and all around him. This inability to penetrate
the continent's interior is a symptom of the larger problem with
interiors and exteriors in the book. Marlow is unable to see into
the interior selves of those around him; instead, he, like the doctor
he visits before he departs for Africa, must base his knowledge on
exterior signs. At the beginning of *Heart of Darkness,* the unnamed
narrator discusses the fact that for Marlow the meaning of a story
or an episode lies in its exterior rather than in any kernel of meaning at its heart. Throughout the book Marlow is indeed confronted
with a series of exteriors, of which travel on the river is a prominent
example. The caravan that goes from the Outer Station to the Central Station provides Marlow with his only opportunity for travel
inland, and he finds there only a depopulated waste scattered with
a few corpses: it tells him nothing. At the very least, travel by river
lays before Marlow a surface to interpret.

3. *Marlow constantly uses vague and often redundant phrases like "unspeakable secrets" and "inconceivable mystery." At other times, however, he is capable of powerful imagery and considerable eloquence. Why does Marlow use vague and "inconclusive" language so frequently?*

In its treatment of imperialism and individual experience, *Heart of Darkness* is on many levels a story about ambiguity. Thus, Marlow's use of language is at the very least thematic. Throughout the book, words assume a bizarre, almost fetishistic power: "ivory," for example, becomes almost more concrete than the elephant tusks themselves. The name "Kurtz" also takes on a life of its own, as it comes to stand for a set of legends and rumors rather than an actual man. Marlow becomes suspicious of words, as they threaten to overtake and distort the meaning they are supposed to convey. On the one hand, words fail to reflect reality adequately, and reality is often so paradoxical that the words don't exist to describe it; but, on the other hand, words sometimes take on an independent life of their own. Marlow's vague terminology, in addition to possessing a lyrical beauty, helps him to negotiate the dual threats of language.

How to Write
Literary Analysis

The Literary Essay: A Step-by-Step Guide

When you read for pleasure, your only goal is enjoyment. You might find yourself reading to get caught up in an exciting story, to learn about an interesting time or place, or just to pass time. Maybe you're looking for inspiration, guidance, or a reflection of your own life. There are as many different, valid ways of reading a book as there are books in the world.

When you read a work of literature in an English class, however, you're being asked to read in a special way: you're being asked to perform *literary analysis*. To analyze something means to break it down into smaller parts and then examine how those parts work, both individually and together. Literary analysis involves examining all the parts of a novel, play, short story, or poem—elements such as character, setting, tone, and imagery—and thinking about how the author uses those elements to create certain effects.

A literary essay isn't a book review: you're not being asked whether or not you liked a book or whether you'd recommend it to another reader. A literary essay also isn't like the kind of book report you wrote when you were younger, where your teacher wanted you to summarize the book's action. A high school- or college-level literary essay asks, "How does this piece of literature actually work?" "How does it do what it does?" and, "Why might the author have made the choices he or she did?"

The Seven Steps
No one is born knowing how to analyze literature; it's a skill you learn and a process you can master. As you gain more practice with this kind of thinking and writing, you'll be able to craft a method that works best for you. But until then, here are seven basic steps to writing a well-constructed literary essay:

1. *Ask questions*
2. *Collect evidence*
3. *Construct a thesis*

4. Develop and organize arguments
5. Write the introduction
6. Write the body paragraphs
7. Write the conclusion

---

1. ASK QUESTIONS

When you're assigned a literary essay in class, your teacher will often provide you with a list of writing prompts. Lucky you! Now all you have to do is choose one. Do yourself a favor and pick a topic that interests you. You'll have a much better (not to mention easier) time if you start off with something you enjoy thinking about. If you are asked to come up with a topic by yourself, though, you might start to feel a little panicked. Maybe you have too many ideas—or none at all. Don't worry. Take a deep breath and start by asking yourself these questions:

- **What struck you?** Did a particular image, line, or scene linger in your mind for a long time? If it fascinated you, chances are you can draw on it to write a fascinating essay.

- **What confused you?** Maybe you were surprised to see a character act in a certain way, or maybe you didn't understand why the book ended the way it did. Confusing moments in a work of literature are like a loose thread in a sweater: if you pull on it, you can unravel the entire thing. Ask yourself why the author chose to write about that character or scene the way he or she did and you might tap into some important insights about the work as a whole.

- **Did you notice any patterns?** Is there a phrase that the main character uses constantly or an image that repeats throughout the book? If you can figure out how that pattern weaves through the work and what the significance of that pattern is, you've almost got your entire essay mapped out.

- **Did you notice any contradictions or ironies?** Great works of literature are complex; great literary essays recognize and explain those complexities. Maybe the title (*Happy Days*) totally disagrees with the book's subject matter (hungry orphans dying in the woods). Maybe the main character acts one way around his family and a completely different way around his friends and associates. If you can find a way to explain a work's contradictory elements, you've got the seeds of a great essay.

At this point, you don't need to know exactly what you're going to say about your topic; you just need a place to begin your exploration. You can help direct your reading and brainstorming by formulating your topic as a *question,* which you'll then try to answer in your essay. The best questions invite critical debates and discussions, not just a rehashing of the summary. Remember, you're looking for something you can *prove or argue* based on evidence you find in the text. Finally, remember to keep the scope of your question in mind: is this a topic you can adequately address within the word or page limit you've been given? Conversely, is this a topic big enough to fill the required length?

GOOD QUESTIONS

"Are Romeo and Juliet's parents responsible for the deaths of their children?"

"Why do pigs keep showing up in LORD OF THE FLIES?*"*

"Are Dr. Frankenstein and his monster alike? How?"

BAD QUESTIONS

"What happens to Scout in TO KILL A MOCKINGBIRD?*"*

"What do the other characters in JULIUS CAESAR *think about Caesar?"*

"How does Hester Prynne in THE SCARLET LETTER *remind me of my sister?"*

---

2. COLLECT EVIDENCE

Once you know what question you want to answer, it's time to scour the book for things that will help you answer the question. Don't worry if you don't know what you want to say yet—right now you're just collecting ideas and material and letting it all percolate. Keep track of passages, symbols, images, or scenes that deal with your topic. Eventually, you'll start making connections between these examples and your thesis will emerge.

Here's a brief summary of the various parts that compose each and every work of literature. These are the elements that you will analyze in your essay, and which you will offer as evidence to support your arguments. For more on the parts of literary works, see the Glossary of Literary Terms at the end of this section.

ELEMENTS OF STORY   These are the *what*s of the work—what happens, where it happens, and to whom it happens.

- **Plot:** All of the events and actions of the work.

- **Character:** The people who act and are acted upon in a literary work. The main character of a work is known as the *protagonist*.

- **Conflict:** The central tension in the work. In most cases, the protagonist wants something, while opposing forces (antagonists) hinder the protagonist's progress.

- **Setting:** When and where the work takes place. Elements of setting include location, time period, time of day, weather, social atmosphere, and economic conditions.

- **Narrator:** The person telling the story. The narrator may straightforwardly report what happens, convey the subjective opinions and perceptions of one or more characters, or provide commentary and opinion in his or her own voice.

- **Themes:** The main idea or message of the work—usually an abstract idea about people, society, or life in general. A work may have many themes, which may be in tension with one another.

ELEMENTS OF STYLE   These are the *how*s—how the characters speak, how the story is constructed, and how language is used throughout the work.

- **Structure and organization:** How the parts of the work are assembled. Some novels are narrated in a linear, chronological fashion, while others skip around in time. Some plays follow a traditional three- or five-act structure, while others are a series of loosely connected scenes. Some authors deliberately leave gaps in their works, leaving readers to puzzle out the missing information. A work's structure and organization can tell you a lot about the kind of message it wants to convey.

- **Point of view:** The perspective from which a story is told. In *first-person point of view*, the narrator involves him or herself in the story. ("I went to the store"; "We watched in horror as the bird slammed into the window.") A first-person narrator is usually the protagonist of the work, but not always. In *third-person point of view*, the narrator does not participate in the story. A third-person narrator may closely follow a specific character, recounting that individual character's thoughts or experiences, or it may be what we call an *omniscient* narrator. Omniscient narrators see and know all: they can witness any event in any time or place and are privy to the inner thoughts and feelings of all characters. Remember that the narrator and the author are not the same thing!

- **Diction:** Word choice. Whether a character uses dry, clinical language or flowery prose with lots of exclamation points can tell you a lot about his or her attitude and personality.

- **Syntax:** Word order and sentence construction. Syntax is a crucial part of establishing an author's narrative voice. Ernest Hemingway, for example, is known for writing in very short, straightforward sentences, while James Joyce characteristically wrote in long, incredibly complicated lines.

- **Tone:** The mood or feeling of the text. Diction and syntax often contribute to the tone of a work. A novel written in short, clipped sentences that use small, simple words might feel brusque, cold, or matter-of-fact.

- **Imagery:** Language that appeals to the senses, representing things that can be seen, smelled, heard, tasted, or touched.

- **Figurative language:** Language that is not meant to be interpreted literally. The most common types of figurative language are *metaphors* and *similes,* which compare two unlike things in order to suggest a similarity between them— for example, "All the world's a stage," or "The moon is like a ball of green cheese." (Metaphors say one thing *is* another thing; similes claim that one thing is *like* another thing.)

3. CONSTRUCT A THESIS

When you've examined all the evidence you've collected and know how you want to answer the question, it's time to write your thesis statement. A *thesis* is a claim about a work of literature that needs to be supported by evidence and arguments. The thesis statement is the heart of the literary essay, and the bulk of your paper will be spent trying to prove this claim. A good thesis will be:

- **Arguable.** "*The Great Gatsby* describes New York society in the 1920s" isn't a thesis—it's a fact.

- **Provable through textual evidence.** "*Hamlet* is a confusing but ultimately very well-written play" is a weak thesis because it offers the writer's personal opinion about the book. Yes, it's arguable, but it's not a claim that can be proved or supported with examples taken from the play itself.

- **Surprising.** "Both George and Lenny change a great deal in *Of Mice and Men*" is a weak thesis because it's obvious. A really strong thesis will argue for a reading of the text that is not immediately apparent.

- **Specific.** "Dr. Frankenstein's monster tells us a lot about the human condition" is *almost* a really great thesis statement, but it's still too vague. What does the writer mean by "a lot"? *How* does the monster tell us so much about the human condition?

GOOD THESIS STATEMENTS

Question: In *Romeo and Juliet*, which is more powerful in shaping the lovers' story: fate or foolishness?

Thesis: "Though Shakespeare defines Romeo and Juliet as 'star-crossed lovers' and images of stars and planets appear throughout the play, a closer examination of that celestial imagery reveals that the stars are merely witnesses to the characters' foolish activities and not the causes themselves."

Question: How does the bell jar function as a symbol in Sylvia Plath's *The Bell Jar*?

Thesis: "A bell jar is a bell-shaped glass that has three basic uses: to hold a specimen for observation, to contain gases, and to maintain a vacuum. The bell jar appears in each of these capacities in *The Bell Jar*, Plath's semi-autobiographical novel, and each appearance marks a different stage in Esther's mental breakdown."

Question: Would Piggy in *The Lord of the Flies* make a good island leader if he were given the chance?

Thesis: "Though the intelligent, rational, and innovative Piggy has the mental characteristics of a good leader, he ultimately lacks the social skills necessary to be an effective one. Golding emphasizes this point by giving Piggy a foil in the charismatic Jack, whose magnetic personality allows him to capture and wield power effectively, if not always wisely."

4. DEVELOP AND ORGANIZE ARGUMENTS

The reasons and examples that support your thesis will form the middle paragraphs of your essay. Since you can't really write your thesis statement until you know how you'll structure your argument, you'll probably end up working on steps 3 and 4 at the same time.

There's no single method of argumentation that will work in every context. One essay prompt might ask you to compare and contrast two characters, while another asks you to trace an image through a given work of literature. These questions require different kinds of answers and therefore different kinds of arguments. Below, we'll discuss three common kinds of essay prompts and some strategies for constructing a solid, well-argued case.

TYPES OF LITERARY ESSAYS

- **Compare and contrast**

    Compare and contrast the characters of Huck and Jim in THE ADVENTURES OF HUCKLEBERRY FINN.

    Chances are you've written this kind of essay before. In an academic literary context, you'll organize your arguments the same way you would in any other class. You can either go *subject by subject* or *point by point*. In the former, you'll discuss one character first and then the second. In the latter, you'll choose several traits (attitude toward life, social status, images and metaphors associated with the character) and devote a paragraph to each. You may want to use a mix of these two approaches—for example, you may want to spend a paragraph a piece broadly sketching Huck's and Jim's personalities before transitioning into a paragraph or two that describes a few key points of comparison. This can be a highly effective strategy if you want to make a counterintuitive argument—that, despite seeming to be totally different, the two objects being compared are actually similar in a very important way (or vice versa). Remember that your essay should reveal something fresh or unexpected about the text, so think beyond the obvious parallels and differences.

- **Trace**

    Choose an image—for example, birds, knives, or eyes—and trace that image throughout MACBETH.

Sounds pretty easy, right? All you need to do is read the play, underline every appearance of a knife in *Macbeth*, and then list them in your essay in the order they appear, right? Well, not exactly. Your teacher doesn't want a simple catalog of examples. He or she wants to see you make *connections* between those examples—that's the difference between summarizing and analyzing. In the *Macbeth* example above, think about the different contexts in which knives appear in the play and to what effect. In *Macbeth*, there are real knives and imagined knives; knives that kill and knives that simply threaten. Categorize and classify your examples to give them some order. Finally, always keep the overall effect in mind. After you choose and analyze your examples, you should come to some greater understanding about the work, as well as your chosen image, symbol, or phrase's role in developing the major themes and stylistic strategies of that work.

- **Debate**

    Is the society depicted in 1984 *good for its citizens?*

    In this kind of essay, you're being asked to debate a moral, ethical, or aesthetic issue regarding the work. You might be asked to judge a character or group of characters (*Is Caesar responsible for his own demise?*) or the work itself (*Is* JANE EYRE *a feminist novel?*). For this kind of essay, there are two important points to keep in mind. First, don't simply base your arguments on your personal feelings and reactions. Every literary essay expects you to read and analyze the work, so search for evidence in the text. What do characters in *1984* have to say about the government of Oceania? What images does Orwell use that might give you a hint about his attitude toward the government? As in any debate, you also need to make sure that you define all the necessary terms before you begin to argue your case. What does it mean to be a "good" society? What makes a novel "feminist"? You should define your terms right up front, in the first paragraph after your introduction.

    Second, remember that strong literary essays make contrary and surprising arguments. Try to think outside the box. In the *1984* example above, it seems like the obvious answer would be no, the totalitarian society depicted in Orwell's novel is *not* good for its citizens. But can you think of any arguments for the opposite side? Even if your final assertion is that the novel depicts a cruel, repressive, and therefore harmful society, acknowledging and responding to the counterargument will strengthen your overall case.

---

5. Write the Introduction

Your introduction sets up the entire essay. It's where you present your topic and articulate the particular issues and questions you'll be addressing. It's also where you, as the writer, introduce yourself to your readers. A persuasive literary essay immediately establishes its writer as a knowledgeable, authoritative figure.

An introduction can vary in length depending on the overall length of the essay, but in a traditional five-paragraph essay it should be no longer than one paragraph. However long it is, your introduction needs to:

- **Provide any necessary context.** Your introduction should situate the reader and let him or her know what to expect. What book are you discussing? Which characters? What topic will you be addressing?

- **Answer the "So what?" question.** Why is this topic important, and why is your particular position on the topic noteworthy? Ideally, your introduction should pique the reader's interest by suggesting how your argument is surprising or otherwise counterintuitive. Literary essays make unexpected connections and reveal less-than-obvious truths.

- **Present your thesis.** This usually happens at or very near the end of your introduction.

- **Indicate the shape of the essay to come.** Your reader should finish reading your introduction with a good sense of the scope of your essay as well as the path you'll take toward proving your thesis. You don't need to spell out every step, but you do need to suggest the organizational pattern you'll be using.

Your introduction should not:

- **Be vague.** Beware of the two killer words in literary analysis: *interesting* and *important*. Of course the work, question, or example is interesting and important—that's why you're writing about it!

- **Open with any grandiose assertions.** Many student readers think that beginning their essays with a flamboyant statement such as, "Since the dawn of time, writers have been fascinated with the topic of free will," makes them sound important and commanding. You know what? It actually sounds pretty amateurish.

- **Wildly praise the work.** Another typical mistake student writers make is extolling the work or author. Your teacher doesn't need to be told that "Shakespeare is perhaps the greatest writer in the English language." You can mention a work's reputation in passing—by referring to *The Adventures of Huckleberry Finn* as "Mark Twain's enduring classic," for example—but don't make a point of bringing it up unless that reputation is key to your argument.

- **Go off-topic.** Keep your introduction streamlined and to the point. Don't feel the need to throw in all kinds of bells and whistles in order to impress your reader—just get to the point as quickly as you can, without skimping on any of the required steps.

---

6. WRITE THE BODY PARAGRAPHS

Once you've written your introduction, you'll take the arguments you developed in step 4 and turn them into your body paragraphs. The organization of this middle section of your essay will largely be determined by the argumentative strategy you use, but no matter how you arrange your thoughts, your body paragraphs need to do the following:

- **Begin with a strong topic sentence.** Topic sentences are like signs on a highway: they tell the reader where they are and where they're going. A good topic sentence not only alerts readers to what issue will be discussed in the following paragraph but also gives them a sense of what argument will be made *about* that issue. "Rumor and gossip play an important role in *The Crucible*" isn't a strong topic sentence because it doesn't tell us very much. "The community's constant gossiping creates an environment that allows false accusations to flourish" is a much stronger topic sentence— it not only tells us *what* the paragraph will discuss (gossip) but *how* the paragraph will discuss the topic (by showing how gossip creates a set of conditions that leads to the play's climactic action).

- **Fully and completely develop a single thought.** Don't skip around in your paragraph or try to stuff in too much material. Body paragraphs are like bricks: each individual one needs to be strong and sturdy or the entire structure will collapse. Make sure you have really proven your point before moving on to the next one.

- **Use transitions effectively.** Good literary essay writers know that each paragraph must be clearly and strongly linked to the material around it. Think of each paragraph as a response to the one that precedes it. Use transition words and phrases such as *however, similarly, on the contrary, therefore,* and *furthermore* to indicate what kind of response you're making.

---

7. WRITE THE CONCLUSION

Just as you used the introduction to ground your readers in the topic before providing your thesis, you'll use the conclusion to quickly summarize the specifics learned thus far and then hint at the broader implications of your topic. A good conclusion will:

- **Do more than simply restate the thesis.** If your thesis argued that *The Catcher in the Rye* can be read as a Christian allegory, don't simply end your essay by saying, "And that is why *The Catcher in the Rye* can be read as a Christian allegory." If you've constructed your arguments well, this kind of statement will just be redundant.

- **Synthesize the arguments, not summarize them.** Similarly, don't repeat the details of your body paragraphs in your conclusion. The reader has already read your essay, and chances are it's not so long that they've forgotten all your points by now.

- **Revisit the "So what?" question.** In your introduction, you made a case for why your topic and position are important. You should close your essay with the same sort of gesture. What do your readers know now that they didn't know before? How will that knowledge help them better appreciate or understand the work overall?

- **Move from the specific to the general.** Your essay has most likely treated a very specific element of the work—a single character, a small set of images, or a particular passage. In your conclusion, try to show how this narrow discussion has wider implications for the work overall. If your essay on *To Kill a Mockingbird* focused on the character of Boo Radley, for example, you might want to include a bit in your conclusion about how he fits into the novel's larger message about childhood, innocence, or family life.

- **Stay relevant.** Your conclusion should suggest new directions of thought, but it shouldn't be treated as an opportunity to pad your essay with all the extra, interesting ideas you came up with during your brainstorming sessions but couldn't fit into the essay proper. Don't attempt to stuff in unrelated queries or too many abstract thoughts.

- **Avoid making overblown closing statements.** A conclusion should open up your highly specific, focused discussion, but it should do so without drawing a sweeping lesson about life or human nature. Making such observations may be part of the point of reading, but it's almost always a mistake in essays, where these observations tend to sound overly dramatic or simply silly.

A+ Essay Checklist

Congratulations! If you've followed all the steps we've outlined above, you should have a solid literary essay to show for all your efforts. What if you've got your sights set on an A+? To write the kind of superlative essay that will be rewarded with a perfect grade, keep the following rubric in mind. These are the qualities that teachers expect to see in a truly A+ essay. How does yours stack up?

- ✓ Demonstrates a thorough understanding of the book
- ✓ Presents an original, compelling argument
- ✓ Thoughtfully analyzes the text's formal elements
- ✓ Uses appropriate and insightful examples
- ✓ Structures ideas in a logical and progressive order
- ✓ Demonstrates a mastery of sentence construction, transitions, grammar, spelling, and word choice

SUGGESTED ESSAY TOPICS

1. Why does HEART OF DARKNESS have two competing heroes? Make the case for either Marlow or Kurtz as the true "hero" of the book.

2. Discuss the framing story that structures HEART OF DARKNESS. Why is it important to narrate Marlow in the act of telling his story?

3. Interpret Kurtz's dying words ("The horror! The horror!"). What do they mean? What are the possible "horrors" to which he is referring? Why is Marlow the recipient of Kurtz's last words?

4. Describe the use of "darkness" both in the book's title and as a symbol throughout the text. What does darkness represent? Is its meaning constant or does it change?

5. How does physical illness relate to madness? How does one's environment relate to one's mental state in this book?

6. Why does Marlow lie to Kurtz's fiancée about Kurtz's last words? Why not tell her the truth, or tell her that Kurtz had no last words, rather than affirming her sentimental and mundane ideas?

A+ STUDENT ESSAY

> Compare Kurtz's African mistress with his Intended. How
> does the pairing of these two women develop larger themes
> in the novel?

On the surface, Kurtz's African mistress has nothing in common
with his Intended. They dress and communicate differently, and
they take on the opposing feminine roles of fiancée and "other
woman." However, despite coming from vastly different cultures,
both women exhibit a fundamental similarity: They exist not so
much as characters in their own right, but as reflections of the man
they share. Conrad emphasizes this connection by referring to each
woman according to her relationship with Kurtz, rather than grant-
ing her an individual name. On one level, Conrad may be suggesting that women inherently play subordinate roles in men's lives.
But on another level, Conrad uses Kurtz's African mistress and
his Intended to attack the very notion that Africa can be seen as
Europe's opposite.

Kurtz's African mistress and his Intended differ in superficial
ways. The African mistress wears bold colors, stripes and fringes,
brass rings that climb up her ankles, and jewelry that Marlow
can only describe as "barbarous" and "bizarre." By contrast,
the Intended presents herself in a way that suggests decorum and
restraint. She appears in the black garb of mourning, with a face
whose paleness contrasts starkly with the bright red paint on the
mistress's cheek. The mistress communicates by way of wordless
gestures and screams, whereas the Intended speaks in calm, thought-
ful, and eloquent sentences. The mistress strikes Marlow and the
other men as scandalous and un-Christian, whereas the very phrase
"the Intended" bears Victorian connotations of modesty, chivalry,
and propriety.

Despite these striking differences, the African mistress and the
Intended share a prominent function in the novel. Both exist primarily to symbolize Kurtz's status and wealth. The mistress's regal pos-
ture, beauty, and excessive jewelry declare to all her countrymen the
fact of Kurtz's brilliance and power. Likewise, the Intended can only
state and repeat Kurtz's vague claims to genius, to the extent that
Marlow becomes irritated. Without Kurtz, the women are merely
"apparitions"—a term that Marlow uses to describe the African

mistress. Separated from Kurtz, the mistress surrenders herself to the gunfire of the Pilgrims, and the Intended becomes a chattering, deluded fool. The two women exist only to proclaim Kurtz's greatness; when that role is removed, they lose their purpose and their usefulness.

By emphasizing the fundamental similarities between a white woman bound by a traditional engagement and an African woman living in supposed sin, Conrad builds on a series of false dichotomies, or opposing pairs. Throughout the novel, he presents us with alleged oppositions that turn out to be disconcertingly similar. Europe, for example, was once as "primitive" as the nineteenth-century Europeans' image of Africa. As Marlow notes, the Pilgrims exhibit many of the savage tendencies of the cannibals. Again and again, the image of blinding sunlight becomes entangled with the image of darkness: Both conditions hamper our ability to see things clearly. Powerless, ignorant, and tragic, the African mistress and the Intended belong to this large set of false dichotomies.

Conrad's two superficially different female characters illustrate his idea that Europe is not the moral and cultural opposite of Africa. With their varied styles of dress and communication, the women initially seem to come from different worlds. But Conrad shows that they are doubles, both confined to the role of displaying Kurtz's power. By exposing the shared tragedy of the two women's lives, Conrad builds on his theme of Victorian moral confusion. Just as Europe is not significantly more advanced than Africa, a refined white woman is not significantly more enlightened than an African "savage."

GLOSSARY OF LITERARY TERMS

ANTAGONIST

The entity that acts to frustrate the goals of the *protagonist*. The antagonist is usually another *character* but may also be a non-human force.

ANTIHERO / ANTIHEROINE

A *protagonist* who is not admirable or who challenges notions of what should be considered admirable.

CHARACTER

A person, animal, or any other thing with a personality that appears in a *narrative*.

CLIMAX

The moment of greatest intensity in a text or the major turning point in the *plot*.

CONFLICT

The central struggle that moves the *plot* forward. The conflict can be the *protagonist*'s struggle against fate, nature, society, or another person.

FIRST-PERSON POINT OF VIEW

A literary style in which the *narrator* tells the story from his or her own *point of view* and refers to himself or herself as "I." The narrator may be an active participant in the story or just an observer.

HERO / HEROINE

The principal *character* in a literary work or *narrative*.

IMAGERY

Language that brings to mind sense-impressions, representing things that can be seen, smelled, heard, tasted, or touched.

MOTIF

A recurring idea, structure, contrast, or device that develops or informs the major *themes* of a work of literature.

NARRATIVE

A story.

NARRATOR

The person (sometimes a *character*) who tells a story; the *voice* assumed by the writer. The narrator and the author of the work of literature are not the same person.

PLOT

The arrangement of the events in a story, including the sequence in which they are told, the relative emphasis they are given, and the causal connections between events.

POINT OF VIEW

The *perspective* that a *narrative* takes toward the events it describes.

PROTAGONIST

The main *character* around whom the story revolves.

SETTING

The location of a *narrative* in time and space. Setting creates mood or atmosphere.

SUBPLOT

A secondary *plot* that is of less importance to the overall story but may serve as a point of contrast or comparison to the main plot.

SYMBOL

An object, *character,* figure, or color that is used to represent an abstract idea or concept. Unlike an *emblem,* a symbol may have different meanings in different contexts.

SYNTAX

The way the words in a piece of writing are put together to form lines, phrases, or clauses; the basic structure of a piece of writing.

THEME

A fundamental and universal idea explored in a literary work.

TONE

The author's attitude toward the subject or *characters* of a story or poem or toward the reader.

VOICE

An author's individual way of using language to reflect his or her own personality and attitudes. An author communicates voice through *tone, diction,* and *syntax.*

LITERARY ANALYSIS

A NOTE ON PLAGIARISM

Plagiarism—presenting someone else's work as your own—rears its ugly head in many forms. Many students know that copying text without citing it is unacceptable. But some don't realize that even if you're not quoting directly, but instead are paraphrasing or summarizing, *it is plagiarism* unless you cite the source.

Here are the most common forms of plagiarism:

- Using an author's phrases, sentences, or paragraphs without citing the source
- Paraphrasing an author's ideas without citing the source
- Passing off another student's work as your own

How do you steer clear of plagiarism? You should *always* acknowledge all words and ideas that aren't your own by using quotation marks around verbatim text or citations like footnotes and endnotes to note another writer's ideas. For more information on how to give credit when credit is due, ask your teacher for guidance or visit www.sparknotes.com.

REVIEW & RESOURCES

QUIZ

1. *Heart of Darkness* opens in what setting?

    A.   A boat on the Congo River
    B.   A boat on the Thames River
    C.   The Company's offices in Brussels
    D.   The Outer Station

2. Where does Kurtz die?

    A.   At the Inner Station
    B.   In Brussels
    C.   Aboard Marlow's steamer
    D.   In the jungle

3. What does Marlow discover atop the fence posts at the Inner Station?

    A.   Human heads
    B.   Monkey skulls
    C.   Dead infants
    D.   The Company flag

4. The Company trades primarily in

    A.   Gold
    B.   Slaves
    C.   Bananas
    D.   Ivory

5. Which of the following receives Kurtz's "Report" after his death?

    A.   Marlow's aunt
    B.   Kurtz's "Intended"
    C.   A representative of the Company
    D.   A journalist

6. Most of Marlow's adventures take place in

    A.   Kenya
    B.   Rhodesia
    C.   The Congo
    D.   England

7. Which of the following is not something that Marlow gives to the Russian trader?

    A.   Food
    B.   Gun cartridges
    C.   Tobacco
    D.   Shoes

8. What do the men at the Central Station hear about the fate of the Eldorado Exploring Expedition?

    A.   That they have been successful and are returning with lots of ivory
    B.   That the expedition's pack animals are dead
    C.   That the men have been ambushed and killed by natives
    D.   That the expedition has found Kurtz

9. At the end of his "Report" on the natives, Kurtz writes:

    A.   "Exterminate all the brutes!"
    B.   "God help us!"
    C.   "No more death!"
    D.   "God save the King!"

10. What one thing does Marlow need to repair his wrecked steamer?

    A.   Steel plates
    B.   A new boiler
    C.   Tools
    D.   Rivets

11. Which of the following does not accompany Marlow on his journey up the river from the Central Station?

    A. The chief accountant
    B. The general manager
    C. The cannibals
    D. The pilgrims

12. How does Marlow's helmsman die?

    A. He is killed and eaten by the cannibals.
    B. He is shot by an angry pilgrim.
    C. He is impaled on a spear thrown from the riverbank.
    D. He falls overboard and drowns.

13. The Company is

    A. English
    B. French
    C. Dutch
    D. Belgian

14. At the Company's offices Marlow encounters

    A. Kurtz
    B. Kurtz's fiancée
    C. Two old women knitting
    D. A Russian trader

15. Why are the cannibals aboard the steamer hungry?

    A. The pilgrims threw their rotting meat overboard.
    B. There are no humans for them to eat.
    C. They have no way to make a fire to cook their food.
    D. They are fasting for religious reasons.

16. Who is ultimately responsible for the attack on the steamer?

    A. The Russian trader
    B. The general manager
    C. Kurtz
    D. Marlow

17. Marlow's predecessor with the Company dies as a result of a quarrel over

A.   Ivory
B.   Hens
C.   A card game
D.   A woman

18. The last person Marlow sees in Brussels is

A.   The president of the Company
B.   His aunt
C.   Kurtz's cousin
D.   Kurtz's fiancée

19. Who helps Marlow to get a job with the Company?

A.   Kurtz
B.   The Director of Companies
C.   His father
D.   His aunt

20. What does the Russian trader leave downriver for the approaching steamer?

A.   Firewood
B.   Water
C.   A map
D.   Food

21. Before he goes to Africa, Marlow has been on a voyage through

A.   The South Pacific
B.   Asia
C.   Central America
D.   Alaska

22. Where does Marlow encounter the "grove of death"?

A.   Brussels
B.   The Outer Station
C.   The Central Station
D.   The Inner Station

23. The chief accountant's most notable characteristic is

    A.   His bald head
    B.   His spotless white clothing
    C.   His shining black shoes
    D.   His unusual hat

24. At the Central Station the native laborers burn

    A.   A hut full of trade goods
    B.   Marlow's steamer
    C.   The chief accountant's quarters
    D.   The surrounding forest

25. What are Kurtz's last words?

    A.   "Exterminate all the brutes!"
    B.   "The horror! The horror!"
    C.   His fiancée's name
    D.   "God help me!"

SUGGESTIONS FOR FURTHER READING

ACHEBE, CHINUA. "'An Image of Africa': Racism in Conrad's *Heart of Darkness.*" In HEART OF DARKNESS: *An Authoritative Text, Backgrounds and Sources, Criticism,* ed. Robert Kimbrough. New York: W. W. Norton & Company, 1988.

BLOOM, HAROLD, ed. *Marlow.* New York: Chelsea House Publishers, 1992.

CHENG, YUAN-JUNG. *Heralds of the Postmodern: Madness and Fiction in Conrad, Woolf, and Lessing.* New York: Peter Lang Publishing, 1999.

EAGLETON, TERRY. *Criticism and Ideology: A Study in Marxist Literary Theory.* London: Verso, reprint edtion 2006.

FIRCHOW, PETER EDGERLY. *Envisioning Africa: Racism and Imperialism in Conrad's* HEART OF DARKNESS. Lexington, KY: University Press of Kentucky, 2000.

GUETTI, JAMES L. *The Limits of Metaphor: A Study of Melville, Conrad, and Faulkner.* Ithaca, NY: Cornell University Press, 1967.

NAVARETTE, SUSAN J. *The Shape of Fear: Horror and the Fin-de-Siecle Culture of Decadence.* Lexington, KY: University Press of Kentucky, 1998.

STAPE, J. H., ed. *The Cambridge Companion to Joseph Conrad.* Cambridge, UK: Cambridge University Press, 1996.

SparkNotes Literature Guides

1984
The Adventures of
  Huckleberry Finn
The Adventures of
  Tom Sawyer
The Aeneid
All Quiet on the
  Western Front
And Then There Were
  None
Angela's Ashes
Animal Farm
Anna Karenina
Anne of Green Gables
Anthem
As I Lay Dying
The Awakening
The Bean Trees
Beloved
Beowulf
Billy Budd
Black Boy
Bless Me, Ultima
The Bluest Eye
Brave New World
The Brothers
  Karamazov
The Call of the Wild
Candide
The Canterbury Tales
Catch-22
The Catcher in the Rye
The Chocolate War
The Chosen
Cold Sassy Tree
The Color Purple
The Count of Monte
  Cristo
Crime and Punishment
The Crucible
Cry, the Beloved
  Country
Cyrano de Bergerac
David Copperfield
Death of a Salesman
Death of Socrates
Diary of a Young Girl

A Doll's House
Don Quixote
Dr. Faustus
Dr. Jekyll and Mr. Hyde
Dracula
Edith Hamilton's
  Mythology
Emma
Ethan Frome
Fahrenheit 451
A Farewell to Arms
The Fellowship of the
  Rings
Flowers for Algernon
For Whom the Bell
  Tolls
The Fountainhead
Frankenstein
The Giver
The Glass Menagerie
The Good Earth
The Grapes of Wrath
Great Expectations
The Great Gatsby
Grendel
Gulliver's Travels
Hamlet
The Handmaid's Tale
Hard Times
Heart of Darkness
Henry IV, Part I
Henry V
Hiroshima
The Hobbit
The House on Mango
  Street
I Know Why the Caged
  Bird Sings
The Iliad
The Importance of
  Being Earnest
Inferno
Invisible Man
Jane Eyre
Johnny Tremain
The Joy Luck Club
Julius Caesar

The Jungle
The Killer Angels
King Lear
The Last of the
  Mohicans
Les Misérables
A Lesson Before Dying
Little Women
Lord of the Flies
Macbeth
Madame Bovary
The Merchant of
  Venice
A Midsummer Night's
  Dream
Moby-Dick
Much Ado About
  Nothing
My Ántonia
Narrative of the Life of
  Frederick Douglass
Native Son
The New Testament
Night
The Odyssey
Oedipus Plays
Of Mice and Men
The Old Man and
  the Sea
The Old Testament
Oliver Twist
The Once and Future
  King
One Flew Over the
  Cuckoo's Nest
One Hundred Years of
  Solitude
Othello
Our Town
The Outsiders
Paradise Lost
The Pearl
The Picture of Dorian
  Gray
Poe's Short Stories
A Portrait of the Artist
  as a Young Man

Pride and Prejudice
The Prince
A Raisin in the Sun
The Red Badge of
  Courage
The Republic
The Return of the King
Richard III
Robinson Crusoe
Romeo and Juliet
Scarlet Letter
A Separate Peace
Silas Marner
Sir Gawain and the
  Green Knight
Slaughterhouse-Five
Song of Solomon
The Sound and the
  Fury
The Stranger
A Streetcar Named
  Desire
The Sun Also Rises
A Tale of Two Cities
The Taming of the
  Shrew
The Tempest
Tess of the
  d'Urbervilles
The Things They
  Carried
The Two Towers
Their Eyes Were
  Watching God
Things Fall Apart
To Kill a Mockingbird
Treasure Island
Twelfth Night
Ulysses
Uncle Tom's Cabin
Walden
War and Peace
Wuthering Heights
A Yellow Raft in Blue
  Water

Visit sparknotes.com for many more!